CARNIVORE KETO

Cookbook

for

A Meat-Based approach to losing weight on a Keto Diet with Tasty Carnivore Recipes

By

Christiana Hills

INTRODUCTION

Of all the diet trends, the carnivore diet may seem like the most radical one. It is one thing to recommend cutting carbs like the ketogenic diet but suggesting that cutting carbs while eating only animal foods are all you need to be healthy and that vegetables can actually be detrimental if not consumed in meager quantity sounds unconventional. But that's the truth and it summarizes everything about the Carnivore diet.

For the same reasons people try a Ketogenic diet: Weight Loss, Cardiovascular Disease, Type 2 Diabetes Management + Blood Sugar Control, Brain Health and a simple approach to eating that lets them consume foods they enjoy, carnivore diet in addition, through scrapping of plant foods minimizes nearly all of the allergens and anti-nutrients that cause health problem and discomfort.

The Keto meets Carnivore diet is a special version that technically combines the merits of the 2 diets. Mostly meat keto is one of the best ways to do the keto diet without getting sucked into the 'keto junk food' trap. It is also a great way to transition to carnivore, whether you're coming from keto, the standard American diet, or something in between.

In this diet, most of your carbs coming from animal products while some specific plant foods are still used as condiments, and sometimes side dishes.

Mostly meat keto contains meat (or eggs) as your main dish, but you may also include a small side of specific vegetables, a sprinkle here and there of your favorite topping etc.

The book contains over 135 recipes with nutritional information to help lose weight while optimizing your health and mental conditions

The scrumptious recipes are classified in Appetizers Breakfast and Main Dishes very easy to make and will help you lose weight while nourishing your body

THE CARNIVORE DIET

The carnivore diet, also called the zero-carb diet, allows foods that come from animals only. There are no 'carnivore police', and of course you are free to eat what you want to eat, but in general the carnivore diet will include:

- ❖ Meat from any animal, including organ meats and bone broth. Meat can be cooked in any way (Instant Pot, slow cooked, grilled, etc)
- ❖ Eggs from any animal including chicken, duck, goose, quail.
- ❖ Dairy, for some people, especially high fat dairy.
- ❖ Honey, which some include on carnivore.
- ❖ Salt and other electrolytes (potassium, magnesium). Historically salt has been a prized commodity, and it is necessary for most people. who are starting out on the carnivore diet

Most people who do the carnivore diet also enjoy the benefits of being in ketosis and a diet where most of the calories come from fat. Dairy is naturally high in fat, and when it is aged (such as cheese) it is lower in carbohydrate. Favorites include: Butter, heavy whipping cream, cheese, and cultured cream.

TOP FOODS TO BE CONSUMED ON A CARNIVORE DIET

Red Meat	Beef, pork, lamb, wild game, birds
White Meat	Chicken, turkey, fish, seafood, sashimi sushi
Organ Meat	Liver, kidneys, tongue, heart, brain
Animal Fat	Bone marrow, tallow
Eggs	Chicken eggs, goose eggs, duck eggs

VARIANT OF THE CARNIVORE DIET

Whether you are eating just meat and salt, or including everything from meat to dairy to eggs and even some seasonings, we detail what different versions of the carnivore diet here.

MEAT AND SALT

This version of the carnivore diet includes meat, salt, water, and that is it. Supplementation with magnesium and potassium is also often helpful. Black coffee and black or green tea can be included if desired. Purists will avoid coffee and tea as well.

Fat is encouraged because when we avoid carbohydrates, the majority of our energy comes from fat. People typically find they feel best when getting at least 70% of their calories from fat, rather than the majority of their calories from protein. Individual needs and preferences may vary.

Salt is used to season, but even black pepper and herbs are avoided. Some autoimmune conditions are sensitive to spices including black pepper, so we really are giving our bodies a break.

Foods eaten when eating that the Meat & Salt version of the carnivore diet:

- Beef, especially fatty cuts
- Chicken, skin on and mostly dark meat for the best satiety
- Lamb
- Seafood including wild-caught shellfish
- Fish, especially fatty fish like salmon
- Pork if desired – some will want to avoid as pork can be hard for some people to digest.
- Meat stock or bone broth made with bones, marrow blended in or eaten separately.
- Organ meat including liver, kidney, sweetbreads, heart, fish eggs, and more from any animal.
- Any other uncured unseasoned meat including pork rinds seasoned only with sea salt, or jerky made with just sea salt and meat.
- Sea Salt

MEAT AND EGGS

The Meat and Eggs version of the carnivore diet includes meat, eggs, and salt, and that is it. As with just meat and salt, supplementation with magnesium and potassium is often helpful.

When eating meat and eggs, you want to make sure your eggs are *just eggs* from a shell. Scrambled eggs from restaurants or from a carton often have fillers such as wheat, soybean oil, and cellulose fiber. The problem with these fillers is that those fillers can cause inflammation or contain excess carbs and may make you think that you're having trouble with eggs, when in reality it's just the fillers that you're reacting to.

In this version of the carnivore diet, you can have everything under Meat & Salt plus:

- Eggs of any kind, including chicken, turkey, duck, etc.
- Raw egg yolks. Raw whites can be consumed, but they contain an anti-nutrient that binds to biotin, a B vitamin, so raw egg whites should be limited. Most of the nutrition from eggs are in the yolks anyway.

MEAT, EGGS, AND DAIRY

Dairy is a game-changer when you are on the carnivore diet. Creamy cream cheese, tangy yogurt and sour cream, melty cheddar, and heavy cream all add richness, flavor, and variety to carnivore. Kefir, cultured cream, and yogurt can all add probiotics as well.

Why wouldn't you include dairy in carnivore? Many people have a sensitivity or allergy to dairy. In addition, the mild creamy goodness of dairy makes it easy to over-eat, a problem with those who are doing carnivore for weight loss.

On the carnivore diet it is generally encouraged to use dairy as a condiment, not the main course. Mostly meat is the theme of most people's best version of the carnivore diet.

Foods included in addition to meat and eggs included:

- Homemade probiotic sour cream
- Commercial plain yogurt
- Milk kefir, plain (see the carnivore resource page for cultures)
- Cheese, store bought or homemade
- Colostrum
- Fluid milk, raw preferred
- Ghee and butter
- Heavy cream in coffee or tea

Meat, Dairy, Eggs, and Seasonings (Mostly Meat)

This version of carnivore includes meat, eggs, and salt, and also additional foods for flavor and texture, not for nutrition. Herbs may also be used as supplements.

This version of carnivore does have loads of benefits and is many people's best version of the carnivore diet because it:

- ✓ Keeps insulin low, which reduces hunger, promotes a healthy weight, and many more benefits.
- ✓ Keeps blood glucose stable, without big highs and lows.
- ✓ Provides variety and seasonings. If you grew up eating heavily seasoned foods, you may find spices harder to give up than sugar! In this version you can keep them in.
- ✓ Makes going out to eat easier. Without having to inspect every ingredient in every food, you can just choose meat, dairy, and eggs from the menu or when eating as a guest without having to cart your own plain meat-and-salt everywhere.

This version of carnivore represents the most liberal version of the carnivore diet, and is a great entry to carnivore. Many people find that a 'mostly meat' version of carnivore, that still includes other zero-carb foods as indicated here is the easiest version of the carnivore diet for them to stick with.

Others find that this version is not restrictive enough and opt to eliminate some or all seasonings.

Common seasonings and sauces to eliminate:

- ✓ Sugar in all forms
- ✓ Nightshades
- ✓ Black pepper
- ✓ Food additives
- ✓ Vegetable oils of any kind (mayo, marinades).
- ✓ Foods included in addition to meat, dairy, and egg on the Meat, Dairy, Eggs, and Seasonings version of the Carnivore Diet:
- ✓ Herbs for flavor such as basil, chives, garlic, etc
- ✓ Spices such as black pepper, turmeric, cinnamon, and ginger
- ✓ Sauces as desired: Mayo, ketchup, mustard, BBQ sauce, etc.

MOSTLY MEAT KETO

This is the version we will be focusing on; it is technically a combination of 2 diets. Mostly meat keto is one of the best ways to do the keto diet without getting sucked into the 'keto junk food' trap. Mostly meat keto is also a great way to transition to carnivore, whether you're coming from keto, the standard American diet, or something in between.

Mostly meat keto, as with most versions of carnivore, has most of your calories coming from animal products. However, plant foods are still used as condiments, and sometimes side dishes.

Mostly meat keto contains meat (or eggs) as your main dish, but you may also include a small side of green vegetables, a sprinkle here and there of nuts, caramelized onions on your burgers, sauerkraut and pickles, etc.

This version of keto makes it very easy to stay under 20-30 g of carb a day, with most people logging in well under 15 g of carbohydrate a day when they stick with eating mostly meat keto-friendly meals.

BENEFITS OF AN ALL MEAT DIET

There are lots of positive testimonials of how people are feeling better or seeing a positive change in their health within 30 days of eating this way.

- Simple eating plan
- No calorie counting food
- Eat until full
- Aid in weight loss
- Decrease inflammation levels
- Reduce glucose levels spikes
- Problems on an All Meat Diet

COMMON MISTAKES ON THE CARNIVORE DIET

1. Eating too little food (this causes unwanted excessive weight loss or other symptoms)
2. Not drinking enough water (drink to satisfy thirst and avoid dehydration)
3. Not adding salt to food (you can experience same keto flu symptoms on this diet too)
4. Eating a moderate all meat diet with added fruits, vegetables & other types of carbs
5. Avoiding fatty meats (don't fear the cholesterol it is good for you)

WHERE TO BUY MEAT

- Your local butcher shop (great place to learn & discuss anything meat)
- Local grocery stores of supermarket
- Local farmers market (great place to meet the farmer & ask questions)
- Order meat online delivered to your home
- Order from Amazon
- Order from US Wellness Meats (Grass Fed Meat Supplier)

SYMPTOMS AND CURES WHEN STARTING THE CARNIVORE DIET

Often, nearly always, when you start a Carnivore Diet, you will experience adverse symptoms and side effects. It is what I affectionately call the "Trough of Despair" or the "Trough" for short. This is the adaptation period.

The symptoms you experience is your body's natural response to carbohydrate restriction and the elimination of addictive agents and chemicals.

Common Symptoms Include:

Brain fog, headache, chills, sore throat, digestive issues, dizziness, irritability, bad breath/smells, bad taste in mouth (metallic), dry mouth, cravings (sugar!), muscle soreness, jaw soreness, nausea, diarrhea, poor focus, and decreased performance, energy, and drive, cramping, rapid heart rate, insomnia, night sweats, and nocturia (peeing a lot at night), hot or cold,

These symptoms are a result of your body undergoing major metabolic and hormonal changes.

The 3 Major Adaptations

If you decide to venture into experimenting with The Carnivore Diet, there are 3 major adaptations that your body is going to undergo.

1. Fluid Rebalancing

Since you are eating fewer carbs, your insulin levels drop, which sends a signal to the kidneys to release sodium from the body.

Losing 10 lbs of water in a couple days is not uncommon as water follows sodium out of the body.

Glycogen is then converted to glucose as the last energy usage before switching to mainly fatty acids.

2. Transitioning from Sugar to Fat for Energy

As your body switches from burning mainly sugar to fat for energy, your body needs to make many modifications on the way.

Your amount of suffering (or lack thereof) depends on your metabolic flexibility. This is your body's ability to adapt to different fuel sources, which depends on a number of factors including genetics, and especially how you ate prior.

If you have been accustomed to eating a lot of high carbohydrate foods, it can feel a lot like giving up other addictions (nicotine, cocaine, etc.)

3. Hormone Response and Rebalancing

As a couple example of hormones responding and rebalancing, let's look at thyroid hormone and cortisol.

Thyroid Hormone Cortisol

T3 thyroid hormone levels may decrease. T3 is a hormone produced by the thyroid that is closely connected with dietary carbohydrates. It plays a major role in regulation of body temperature, metabolism, and heart rate.

You can dramatically lessen and perhaps even eliminate most of the suffering in the "Trough" by using some tricks to help bridge your body to the adapted state of bliss.

4 TRICKS AND TIPS TO LIMIT OR AVOID THE "TROUGH"

1. Eat more meat.

2. Hydrate: Make sure you are drinking water. No need to overdo it (that can exacerbate the situation) but you need to stay hydrated.

3. Electrolytes: As you lose a lot of excess water, you also lose a lot of electrolytes: sodium, potassium, magnesium, chloride. Supplemental electrolytes can help immensely. Salt used generously on your meat is a good Step

4. Sleep

As someone who has treated many patients with sleep disorders, I can tell you one thing for certain, if you get good shut eye, everything else in your life will be better.

Insomnia is common during adaptation, and since you are purging water, nocturia is also an interrupter. A few hacks that help:

WHAT IS THE KETOGENIC DIET AND HOW DOES IT WORK?

The ketogenic diet is a low-carbohydrate, high-fat diet. It's kind of similar to other low-carb diets like Atkins, but instead of replacing carbs with protein, you add in a ton of fat. This sends the body into ketosis, where we start burning fat as our primary source of energy.

The ketogenic diet has actually been around for almost a century. It was initially developed in the 1920s to treat epilepsy and has since been used to help with weight loss, cardiovascular health, diabetes, brain disorders and certain types of cancer.

A QUICK REVIEW OF FATS

Fat is an important macronutrient that has unfortunately been vilified for decades. Emerging research shows that all of the low-fat advice we grew up with was unfounded and fat doesn't lead to obesity and heart disease.

THE ROLE OF FAT IN THE BODY:

- Helps form our cell membranes
- Offers us a rich source of energy
- Protects our nervous system
- Helps us make hormones
- Forms our brains
- Supports effective functioning of the nervous system
- Nourishes our skin from the inside out
- Stabilizes blood sugar levels
- Lubricates our joints

All crucial stuff, right? So you can see why eliminating it could potentially cause us harm, while eating more of it can benefit our health and wellness.

HOW DID THE KETOGENIC (KETO) DIET BECOME POPULAR?

As I mentioned, the keto diet was initially used by doctors to treat epilepsy, particularly in children. The diet waned from the 1970s onwards (likely due to the belief that high fat diets were at the root of heart disease- a theory that has since been disproven). The diet was brought to the forefront again in 2000 when an episode of Dateline featured the story of a little boy suffering from epilepsy - and the medications weren't working. His seizures became so bad his parents turned to the ketogenic diet as a last resort and it cured him completely. (His parents went on to found a non-profit organization and direct a TV movie about their son that starred Merryl Streep.)

After that, scientists found a renewed interest in the ketogenic diet and began to explore it in more detail through clinical studies. What they found was substantial!

THE HEALTH BENEFITS OF THE KETOGENIC DIET

The ketogenic diet has a wide range of crucial health benefits, including:

1. **Weight Loss:** Fat isn't going to make us fat. When we consume the right amount of fat for our bodies, we feel more satisfied and satiated. We don't ride on the blood sugar roller coaster. A number of singular studies (like this one) show that participants on ketogenic diets lose more weight than those on low-fat diets. And they keep it off - this meta-analysis concluded that high-fats diets were better than low-fat ones in the long run.

2. **Cardiovascular Disease:** The weight loss studies I referred to above also examined cardiovascular risk factors. The participants didn't experience negative cardio impacts from eating fat and the meta-analysis found that the keto diet helped to lower blood pressure and raise HDL cholesterol. Another meta-analysis that focused on the keto diet and

heart health concluded that very low-carb diets help to lower blood pressure and LDL cholesterol, raise HDL cholesterol, improve blood vessel function and reduce inflammation.

3. **Type 2 Diabetes Management + Blood Sugar Control:** Eating fat stabilizes our blood sugar levels. In one study comparing the keto diet to the low glycemic index diet, the keto diet group experienced a greater improvement in glycemic control and some participants were even able to reduce their diabetes medications. Other studies show that the keto diet, when compared to low-fat eating, can lower glucose and insulin concentrations and improve insulin sensitivity. In this study of Type 2 diabetes patients, most of the participants were able to eliminate or drastically reduce their meds.

4. **Epilepsy:** The keto diet is considered a valid option as part of treatment for epilepsy, though more so in children than adults. In this study of children with challenging seizures, the kids followed the keto diet for a year. Researchers followed up with the families three years and six years later, discovering that many of the children either decreased or eliminated their medications.

5. **Brain Health:** Our brains are about 60% fat. Emerging evidence indicates that ketone bodies can help improve memory and can potentially treat Alzheimer's disease.

Other areas of research indicate that ketogenic diets may be able to improve acne, symptoms of Parkinson's disease, suppress or reduce cancer tumors, diminish PCOS symptoms, and help heal brain trauma.

IS THE KETOGENIC DIET RIGHT FOR YOU?

We are all biochemically unique, which is why I recommend people work with their favorite natural health care practitioner (this is mine) to ensure they are following a safe ketogenic diet, especially if you have metabolic conditions where medications are concerned.

If you are interested in experimenting with the ketogenic diet, try it for a couple of weeks and see if you notice a difference in your health. We all have different metabolic types, and some of us will feel better than others on a high-fat diet.

This may be stating the obvious, but it's virtually impossible to do this safely if you're vegan. There is only so many nuts, seeds and coconut you can eat, and you probably won't feel satiated or vibrant without the animal side of things. But if you've done it successfully, then let me know!

A ketogenic diet is a diet with so little carbohydrate in it that the body is forced to use fat (instead of sugar) as its primary fuel source. Clearly this has advantages for weight loss, but it apparently has other advantages as well. Since ketogenic diets are by definition high in fat (and moderate in protein), they don't jack blood sugar up, and therefore the demand on the body for insulin is greatly reduced. When insulin is no longer elevated all the time—the way it frequently is on a high-carb diet—the cells begin to regain their sensitivity to insulin and insulin resistance begins to fade. As everyone who reads my columns knows, insulin resistance is a factor in a baker's dozens of degenerative diseases, so anything that increases insulin sensitivity (reducing insulin resistance) is a pretty terrific thing for health and longevity.

Ketones—also known as ketone bodies—are produced as a by-product of fat-burning. And they are a terrific fuel for the heart, the muscles and the brain. And let's remember that cancer cells thrive on sugar—it's really their only fuel.

1. So when you reduce sugar in the diet (and the bloodstream), you're essentially depriving cancer cells of the fuel they need to survive and spread. Ketogenic diets are now being proposed as an adjunctive cancer therapy.

2. Anecdotally, some well-known people in the health and fitness space—namely superstar Hollywood trainer Vinnie Tortorich— have credited a ketogenic diet with keeping their cancer in remission. And noted researcher (and TED lecturer) Terry Wahls, M.D., has pioneered ketogenic diets for multiple sclerosis, plus she is currently conducting

trials of her particular form of the diet—known as the Wahls protocol—
for MS patients.

To summarize, the ketogenic diet is essentially "very low carbohydrate high fat diet" (abbreviated LCHF)–one that produces a state known as nutritional ketosis. People who follow Keto diets usually monitor their ketone levels with devices that allow them to measure ketones in the blood, the urine, or, more recently, through the breath.

BREAKFAST

KETO BREAKFAST SKILLET

Prep Time: 30 minutes || Cook Time: 20 minutes

Servings: 3 people

Calories: 247kcal

Course: Breakfast

Ingredients

- 8 oz Ground Pork Breakfast Sausage
- 1.5 cups radishes
- 1/2 onion medium
- 1/8 tsp Cayenne Pepper or black pepper
- 1/4 tsp salt

Instructions

1. Chop your onions in radishes into small pieces
2. The radishes are taking the place of the potatoes in a traditional breakfast skillet.
3. Cook your pork sausage in a separate skillet and save your grease

How to Make It:

1. Cook your pork sausage and save the grease
2. Combine your chopped onions and radishes into the skillet with your pork grease
3. add your pepper and salt
4. Saute your onions and radishes for 15 – 20 minutes or until tender mixing it often.
5. After your onions and radishes are soft add your sausage back into the skillet and cook with your radishes and onions.
6. Add your 1/4 cup of shredded cheese and let it melt
7. In a separate skillet fry or scramble an egg and add it on top of your skillet mix.
8. Serve and enjoy!

Total Carbs = 4 Grams || Net Carbs = 3 grams

Serving: 4oz | Calories: 247kcal | Carbohydrates: 4g | Protein: 12g | Fat: 20g | Saturated Fat: 7g | Cholesterol: 54mg | Sodium: 698mg | Potassium: 349mg | Fiber: 1g | Sugar: 2g | Vitamin A: 91IU | Vitamin C: 10mg | Calcium: 26mg | Iron: 1mg

KETO BREAKFAST CASSEROLE

Prep Time: 30 minutes ||| Cook Time: 35 minutes

Servings: 12 people

Calories388kcal

Course: Breakfast

This is a delicious and easy to make keto, low carb, carnivore friendly recipe. This recipe is also great for meal prepping as well. Easy, delicious, and versatile a dish that everyone will enjoy!

Equipment

- 9 x 13 Casserole Dish

Ingredients

Casserole Ingredients

- 12 eggs
- 1.5 pounds sausage
- 3/4 cup bacon crumbles or 12 slices
- 3/4 cup heavy cream
- 2 cups grated cheese
- 2 TSP hot sauce

Instructions

1. Preheat oven to 350°. Grease a 9 x 13"casserole baking dish.

2. Crumble and brown sausage. Drain. Warm bacon crumbles with sausage. If using fresh bacon, cook and crumble.
3. Put prepared meats on bottom of casserole. Sprinkle with 1 cup of the grated cheese.
4. Add 12 eggs to a blender, add heavy cream, seasonings if desired, and 2 tablespoons of hot sauce. Blend until fluffy. Alternately whisk in a large bowl.
5. Pour over meats and cheese in casserole dish. Add remaining grated cheese.
6. Bake for 35 to 40 minutes, or until a knife inserted comes out clean.
7. Garnish with onion if desired.

Each piece: 123 grams or 4.33 oz

Each piece was approximately - 3"x 2.5"

Serving: 123g | Calories: 388kcal | Carbohydrates: 1g | Protein: 22g | Fat: 32g | Saturated Fat: 15g | Cholesterol: 255mg | Sodium: 778mg | Potassium: 231mg | Sugar: 1g | Vitamin A: 687IU | Vitamin C: 1mg | Calcium: 175mg | Iron: 2mg

BROWN SUGAR CHICKEN AND WAFFLES

Prep Time: 10 minutes || Cook Time: 25 minutes

Calories: 610kcal

Servings: 4

Course: Breakfast, Main Course

Ingredients

- 1 recipe Buttermilk Waffles
- 1 chicken broken down into 8 pieces, 2 wings, 2 drumsticks, 2 thighs, 2 breasts (breasts can be cut in half for portion size
- 1 cup buttermilk
- 1 tbs Tabasco sauce
- 1 tsp white vinegar
- salt and pepper
- 1-2 cups flour
- 2 tbs brown sugar
- 1 tsp chili powder
- 1/2 tsp cayenne pepper
- Oil for frying

Instructions

1. Whisk the buttermilk, Tabasco, and vinegar together.
2. Place chicken in a resealable bag and pour the buttermilk over top.
3. Allow to marinate 4 to 8 hours in fridge.
4. When ready to cook
5. Prep your waffles and keep them warm in an over set to 300 degrees F.
6. Heat the oil in a large Dutch Oven.
7. Arrange the flour in a shallow dish and whisk in a little salt and pepper.
8. Arrange a baking sheet with a grate set in the middle for drying.
9. Whisk the brown sugar, chili powder, and cayenne in a small bowl and set aside.
10. Remove each piece of chicken from the buttermilk and allow the excess to drain off.
11. Dredge in the flour and make sure to coat all sides.
12. Carefully place a few pieces as a time in the fry for about 15 minutes, until cooked through and golden.
13. Carefully remove chicken to the wire rack for a moment
14. Using tongs, toss in the bowl with the brown sugar mix to coat.
15. Place back on the rack to dry.
16. Repeat as needed for each piece.
17. Serve over the buttermilk waffles with a little syrup on the side.

CARNIVORE TORTILLAS

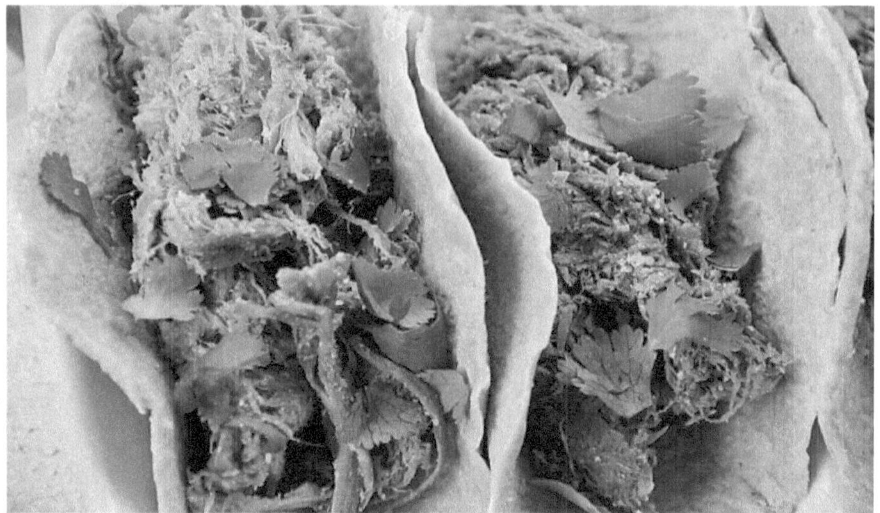

Per 11 tortillas, each tortilla is 1g fat and 4g protein, 0g carbs.

Ingredients

- 4 oz cooked poultry - we used light & dark meat chicken*
- 115g egg whites
- 2 whole eggs
- 1 tsp salt

Directions

1. Add ingredients to a blender and Blend until smooth
2. Coat pan in butter and make sure it's on medium low
3. Spoon two tablespoons worth of batter on the pan and spread into a circle
4. Allow to cook until almost cooked through, flip and cook a little less on the second side
5. Remove from heat, and allow pan to cool to medium low again until greasing and making the next tortilla

CARNIVORE CAKE

Yes, folks, it is here, the beautiful zero carb cake that is 100% carnivore and extra angel like. This carnivore keto cake recipe is light, fluffy, and very easy with only 2 main ingredients.

Ingredients:

- 150g egg whites
- 1/4 tsp cream of tartar (technically optional) *
- 15g egg white protein powder**

Directions:

1. Preheat oven to 375 degrees F
2. Measure out egg whites in a dry bowl (ideally a stand mixer)
3. Add cream of tartar (if using) and whip the egg whites (using stand mixer or manually with a hand mixer - a lot more difficult and doesn't get as stiff - until "stiff peaks" form
4. Gently fold in protein powder and sweetener of choice
5. Grease a baking dish with butter or tallow
6. Spoon fluffed egg white mixture onto baking dish and form into a cake shake
7. Bake in oven for 20-25 minutes, until golden at the top

Optional: sweetener such as stevia, monk fruit extract, or pure glycine powder***
and cinnamon

*Cream of tartar is a byproduct of wine production, you technically do not have to
include this, but cream of tartar does help "floof" up the egg whites, allowing for
stiff peaks to form and for the whites to maintain a fluffy consistency.

**You can use any protein powder, but egg white protein powder does seem to
give the cake a better consistency overall. ***Using pure glycine to sweeten the
cake will keep this cake recipe entirely carnivore. However, if your protein
powder has some sort of sweetener in it, you can omit this step. Totally up to you!
Cinnamon is also optional, but it will just give the cake a nice flavor if you prefer.

Macros for entire recipe: depends on how much egg whites and what protein
powder you are using, but it is roughly 29g protein, 0g carbs & 0g fat.

HOMEMADE RAW BUTTER RECIPE

Ingredients:

- Raw cream from raw milk*
- Optional: Redmond real salt to taste

*You can buy raw cream or you can leave raw milk in the fridge for a few days until the cream separates & you can obtain your own cream.

Directions:

1. If you have raw milk, leave in the fridge until cream visibly separates and then pull cream
2. Blend cream for 5 or so minutes until more of a cottage cheese consistency
3. Knead the butter under cold running water to separate it from the buttermilk
4. Optionally salt, store in fridge & enjoy!

CARNIVORE CHICKEN SKIN CHIPS

Here is officially the perfect snack for any Carnivore missing a crunch in his or her diet. These super crispy, super fatty chicken skin chips are a great, dairy-free alternative to the typical zero carb cheese chips/crisp recipes.

These low carb (no carb) chips are instead loaded with fats and collagen!

Ingredients

- Chicken skin (I bought a whole chicken with skin on)
- Redmond Real Sea Salt

Instructions

1. Peel all skin off chicken, wash the skin, & pat completely dry
2. Cut the skin into chip shapes
3. Place skin on parchment paper & season with Redmond real salt
4. Place another piece of parchment paper on top, and place another baking pan on top to keep them flat when baking
5. Bake at 400F for 10 min
6. Flip & bake for another 8-10 min until crispy

CARNIVORE BURGER

This carnivore burger (+ Keto) is completely customizable and has a zero carb bun and everything. Ain't no carbs on this plate! Since we chose to use a blend of ground bison with liver & heart, the burger patty itself is loaded with nutrients and a great source of both fat and protein.

Ingredients

- Chicken round buns (recipe Below) --> chicken, eggs, baking soda, ACV
- Ground meat (we used ground bison blend with liver & heart from North Star Bison)
- Sea Salt
- Egg
- Bacon
- Tallow

Instructions

1. Make the chicken round buns
2. Form burger patty with ground meat & sea salt (optional other seasonings)
3. Cook bacon on a cast iron skillet
4. Save bacon fat on pan, cook burger patty(s) in bacon fat
5. On a separate pan, cook over easy egg (we always cook ours in tallow)

6. Melt tallow in microwave and top 1 side of 2 chicken rounds with melted tallow. This is MAJOR KEY! It'll add extra crunch to the sandwich when it solidifies as a crispy shell
7. Layer 1 chicken round with burger, bacon, over easy egg, and top with second chicken round!
8. Optionally add cheese, but we typically eat dairy free so no cheese on these particular burgers.

CHICKEN ROUNDS

This recipe makes 12 rounds. Perfect for 6 burgers or sammies!

Ingredients

- 1 pound of cooked chicken
- 4 of the finest eggs you can find
- 1/2 tsp baking soda
- 1/2 tsp Apple cider vinegar

Instructions

1. Blend everything in your blender until smooth.
2. Use a spoon to make the rounds on a parchment lined sheet pan. Just shape them into flat circles. They will rise, but just the tiniest amount. They will not spread so you can put them 1-2 inches apart.
3. Bake at 350° for 8-9 minutes. Let cool and enjoy with your favorite meats!

BACON-WRAPPED SCALLOPS

Servings: 2 People

Calories: 225 Kcal

These are like candy on the carnivore diet! So good, and they cook quickly in the oven. For packing lunch, they can be kept warm in a thermos.

Ingredients

- 8 large sea scallops
- 4 slices thin bacon

Instructions

1. Preheat oven to 425*F and line a baking sheet with parchment paper. Cut bacon in half crosswise. Precook bacon for 3-4 minutes flat on the parchment. As the bacon cooks, pat scallops dry with paper towels and set aside.
2. Once bacon has cooled until it's cool enough to touch, wrap bacon around each scallop and secure with a toothpick.
3. Place on baking sheet, and repeat with the remaining scallops. Bake for 12 minutes and then serve warm.

Amount Per Serving (1 serving)

Calories 225Calories from Fat 162, Fat 18g 28%, Saturated Fat 6g 30%, Cholesterol 43mg 14%, Sodium 526mg 22%, Potassium 210mg 6%, Carbohydrates 2g 1%, Protein 13g 26%, Iron 1mg 6%

BBQ RIB HASH

Prep Time: 10 minutes || Cook Time: 25 minutes

Course: Breakfast, Main Course

Servings: 4 servings

Calories: 496kcal

Have leftover ribs? This is the perfect way to use up the pork in a hearty breakfast.

Ingredients

- 1 leftover porked ribs cooked
- 2 russet potatoes scrubbed, chopped and lined on a wire rack to dry for 20 minutes
- 2 tbs Olive oil
- Salt and pepper
- 1 2 red pepper diced
- 1 2 green pepper diced
- 1 4 onion diced
- 8 Eggs
- 8 slices Toast

Instructions

1. Reheat the pork ribs in the oven or on the grill, wrapped in foil, until heated through. Set aside until cool enough to touch and remove meat from bones of half the rack.
2. Slice the remainder at each bone to toss onto the plates if you are feeling rugged, otherwise, chop all the meat.
3. Meanwhile, in a large skillet over medium-high heat, heat the oil to coat the pan. Toss in the potatoes and season with salt and pepper.
4. Cook for 10 minutes, stirring as needed, until starting to soften and crisp a bit. Add the red and green pepper and the onion to the pan and sauté another 10 to 15 minutes, until potatoes are golden and crispy all over.
5. Stir in the chopped rib meat and toss to combine.
6. Meanwhile, in a separate greased pan, fry a couple of eggs to pile high on top as desired and toast and butter some bread.
7. Toss it all together on a platter and serve with a meaty rib for those who are feeling brave enough to take on brunch with a wet-nap.

NOTES

This recipe works great with leftover pork ribs on the bone from any cut, spare to St Louis style. It would also work well with leftover boneless country style ribs too. Or even with leftover beef short ribs.

Hash holds for up to 3 days in the fridge in an airtight container. Reheat in a skillet over low heat, or in the oven over 325 degrees F for 15 minutes on a greased baking sheet.

KETO BUTTER BURGERS

Prep Time: 10 minutes || Cook Time: 10 minutes

Servings: 12

Calories: 125kcal

Course: Breakfast

These Keto Butter Burgers are the ultimate savory fat bomb!

Ingredients

- 1 lb. ground beef (85% lean)
- 3 T butter
- 2 oz cheese (any kind; I used Colby Jack)
- Salt to taste
- Pepper to taste
- Onion powder to taste (optional)
- Garlic powder to taste (optional)

Instructions

1. Preheat oven to 375 degrees.
2. In a medium-sized bowl, combine ground beef with your desired amount of salt and pepper. Optionally, add onion powder and/or garlic powder.
3. Press a small amount of beef (about 1 tbsp.) into the bottom of a non-stick, 12-slot muffin pan so the bottom is fully covered.

4. Add a pat of butter to the top of each piece of beef.
5. Again add beef to the top. Press to flatten.
6. Add a small piece of cheese to the beef.
7. Add a final layer of beef. (It's okay if you don't have quite enough beef left to fully cover the top of the cheese.) Press to flatten.
8. Place the muffin pan in the oven and bake for 10 minutes. **If using a silicone muffin pan, place it on top of a cookie sheet before adding it to the oven!**
9. When the baking is complete, turn OFF the oven and crack the oven door for a few minutes to release the heat. This is to allow the excess oil to cool down.
10. Please be VERY CAREFUL before removing your muffin pan from the oven because the fat from the beef and butter will be very hot.
11. Using a fork, remove each Butter Burger from the pan and place on a plate. (Note: Your burgers should be cooked through; if they're not, return them to the oven for a few minutes.)
12. There will be a delicious beef fat/butter combo remaining in the muffin pan. Save this and use it to drizzle on your Butter Burgers, cook veggies, etc.

Notes

NOTE: If you use a silicone muffin pan, place the pan on a sheet pan to prevent the oil from spilling when you remove the pan from the oven.

Calories 125 Calories from Fat 90, Fat 10g 15%, Saturated Fat 5g 31%, Cholesterol 38mg 13%, Sodium 79 mg3%, Potassium 116mg 3%, Carbohydrates 0g 0%, Sugar 0g 0%, Protein 8g 16%, Vitamin A 135IU 3%, Calcium 41mg 4%, Iron 0.8mg 4%

CARNIVORE'S LASAGNA

Total Time: 2hrs 10mins

Serves: 12

Yield: 1 Lasagna

Ingredients

- 1 tablespoon olive oil
- 2 lbs lean ground beef, divided
- 1 lb. hot Italian sausage, sliced
- ½ onion, chopped
- 4 garlic cloves, crushed
- 3 (15 ounce) cans tomato sauce
- 2 tablespoons brown sugar
- 1 teaspoon fennel seed, divided
- 1 teaspoon dry basil, divided
- 1 teaspoon dried thyme, divided
- 1 teaspoon dry oregano, divided
- 2 teaspoons salt, divided
- 1 teaspoon black pepper, divided
- 2 tablespoons dried parsley, divided
- 2 eggs

- ½ cup oatmeal
- 1 ½ cups parmesan cheese, shredded
- 32 ounces ricotta cheese
- ½ teaspoon ground nutmeg
- 8 -16 ounces mozzarella cheese, shredded
- 2/3 lb. pepperoni, chopped into small pieces
- 18 lasagna noodles

Directions

1. Preheat oven to 350°F.
2. In a heavy pan, heat the olive oil over medium heat. Add the onion, garlic, half of the ground meat, and the Italian sausage. Brown for 10 minutes.
3. Drain the meat mixture, if needed. Add the tomato sauce, brown sugar, 1 tablespoon parsley, and 1/2 teaspoon each of the fennel seed, basil, thyme, oregano, black pepper and salt. Gently stir, cover, and let simmer over low heat for 1 hour.
4. While the sauce is cooking, prepare the meatballs, ricotta cheese mixture, and lasagna noodles. First, beat 1 egg in a large bowl. Add the oatmeal, 1/2 cup of Parmasan, and the rest of the ground meat, black pepper, fennel seed, basil, thyme, oregano, and salt. Combine well.
5. Roll the meat into balls that are about 1 inch in diameter. Place them on a sprayed pan and bake for 20 minutes, turning the meatballs over halfway through the cooking time.
6. Put the ricotta cheese in another bowl. Add the other egg, nutmeg, and rest of parsley. Combine well and set aside.
7. Now just soak the lasagna noodles in a large pan filled with very hot water for at least 15 minutes.
8. Once the sauce is cooked, construct the lasagna in a deep 9x3-inch pan. First, spread 2 cups of the sauce on the bottom of the pan. Lay 6 noodles down. Spread half of the ricotta over the noodles, then sprinkle that with 1/3 of the mozzeralla and parmasan. Top that with half of the pepperoni.
9. Make another layer in the same way, starting with 2 cups of sauce. After that, lay down the rest of the lasagna noodles on top.
10. Mix in the cooked meatballs with the rest of the sauce, and spread on top of the lasagna. Top with rest of cheese.
11. Cover with foil, and bake at 350F for 25 minutes. Remove the foil, then bake for 25 minutes. Remove, then let cool for at least 15 minutes before serving.

CARNIVORE PANCAKE PATTIES

These carnivore pancake patties would be perfect for breakfast, as a side dish, or for dinner. Platta 1, 2, or 3 :) These pancakes are savory and contain only 3 ingredients - breakfast sausage, eggs, & pork rinds.

Ingredients

- 6 oz pasture raised sausage
- 2 eggs
- 1 & 1/4 oz pork rinds (we used Epic brand)

Directions

1. Preheat oven to 375 and prepare baking pan with foil and spray
2. Using a blender or food processor, crush pork rinds into a fine flour
3. Combine the eggs and sausage in a bowl and then stir in the pork rinds
4. Spread into thin circular shapes on sprayed pan
5. Bake for 20-30 minutes (this will depend on how thin your patties are)
6. Allow patties to cool once finished before removing from pan

0 carbs | 5 fat | 5 protein

MACROS per serving (out of 10):

We recommend sourcing your sausage from White Oak Pastures, which raises some of the best pastured pork available.

CARNIVORE CAKE

Prep time: 15 mins || Cook time: 2 hours 30 mins

Serves: 12

Ingredients

Braunschweiger:

- 1 ¼ pounds pork or beef liver
- ½ pound pork shoulder (or beef tongue)
- ¾ pound pork back fat
- 3 teaspoons fine grain sea salt
- 4 hardboiled eggs

DECORATIONS:

- 12 Slices of prosciutto or carpaccio
- 12 slices Pederson's Farms bacon (for Bacon Roses)

Instructions

1. Cut the pork liver, pork shoulder and fat into cubes. Place into a food processor or blender and puree until you have a smooth puree.

2. Pack the puree into a 7-inch (spring-form works best) cake pan and cover tightly with foil making sure the foil lines the pan so the water doesn't get in. Place the pan in a roasting pan with an inch boiling water and bake at 300 degrees F for 2 hours or until meat is cooked but not browned; cook until the internal temperature of the meat reads 160 degrees F.
3. Remove loaf pan from the roasting pan. Use a spoon to 4 egg-sized holes into the meat. Place the hard boiled eggs into the meat and pat the meat back over the eggs. Let it completely cool in the cake pan. Refrigerate 1 to 2 days before using.
4. Remove the Braunschweiger from the cake pan. Prosciutto is often sticky enough to hold to the Braunschweiger. Use your hands to form the prosciutto around the meat cake.
5. Meanwhile make the bacon roses
6. Store in air tight container in the fridge for up to 6 days.

409 calories, 34g fat, 24g protein, 2g carbs, 0g fiber

ZERO CARB KETO CARNIVORE DIET FRENCH FRIES

These zero carb French fries are thick, crispy, and delicious. They are low carb, high protein and are made entirely of animal - healthy, grain free French fries perfect for paleo, keto, & the carnivore diet.

Ingredients

- 4 oz cooked poultry - we used light & dark meat chicken
- 10g pork rinds (we used Epic brand, baked sea salt)
- 1 whole egg
- 1/4 tsp salt
- 1/4 tsp baking powder (optional)

Directions

1. Preheat oven to 350
2. Line baking dish with parchment paper
3. Blend all ingredients until smooth - it will be chunky
4. Stuff blend into a plastic baggie and cut a small hole in a corner so you can 'pipe' out the fries onto the parchment paper
5. Pipe out desired size of fries and then flatten and shape fries
6. Bake in oven for 15-20 minutes
7. Then broil on high for 2-3 minutes until golden and crispy on top
8. Makes about 12-15 thick cut fries

Per serving (around 12-15 thick fries):

Calories: 248, Fat: 10g, Protein: 38g, Carbs: 0g

CARNIVORE DIET MILK SHAKE RECIPE

Keto carnivore milkshake recipe that is thick and creamy! The taste is so rich and this low carb milkshake is made of only 2 main ingredients, no sugar.

Ingredients (2 servings):

- 1.5 cups of carnivore ice cream (225g)
- 1/3 cup of milk (80ml)
- 1/4 tsp salt
- 1/4 tsp vanilla extract*

*Vanilla extract is optional, especially if your ice cream flavor is already vanilla. But, would recommend adding it to enhance the vanilla bean flavor more.

Directions

1. Prepare a batch of carnivore ice cream or pick up your favorite keto ice cream brand
2. Blend together all ingredients until smooth
3. Enjoy!

EASY ZERO CARB VANILLA ICE CREAM

Serving size: 1/2 cup

Yield: 8 servings

Craving ice cream? Whip up a batch of this creamy vanilla ice cream, and have some to enjoy in minutes! If you'd like a different flavor, try switching out the vanilla extract with another, like banana, maple, almond, or pineapple.

Jazz up your freshly made ice cream with optional toppings, such as seedless raspberry jam, blueberry jam, chopped nuts, granola, dark chocolate pieces, shredded coconut, warmed nut butter, or Aunt Lee's Pancake syrup.

Ingredients:

- 3 cups heavy cream
- 1 cup water
- a pinch of salt
- 1 1/3 tbsp. pure vanilla extract
- 5 or more tsp. natural, non-GMO granular erythritol

Directions:

1. Place all the ingredients into a large bowl.
2. Whisk until foamy.
3. Pour the cream mixture into a blender. Using the whip setting on the blender, blend until the mixture resembles whipped cream.
4. Use a rubber spatula to scrape the ice cream base into an ice cream maker.* Use as per manufacturer's instructions to make ice cream.
5. Scoop into dessert bowls, and top with your favorite toppings.

*Note: If you don't have an ice cream maker, you can divide the ice cream base evenly into popsicle molds, and freeze. Alternately, you can scrape the ice cream base into a covered, freezer-safe bowl. Then freeze it, mixing every 1/2 hour until it reaches the desired consistency.

CORNED BEEF & MUSTARD CREAM

A great low carb slow cooker recipe for these winter months, and uses mostly pantry staples.

I'd never had corned beef before and was actually very tender and loved the addition of the mustard cream.

I found this worked well for my style of carnivore - meat and dairy, with basic seasonings.

Ingredients

Corned Beef

- 2kg corned beef silverside (rinsed and pat dry)
- 2 tbsp. olive oil
- 2 tsp onion powder
- 3 tsp minced garlic
- 2 tbsp. thyme leaves
- 3 fresh bay leaves
- 1 tbsp. Whole Peppercorns
- 1/4 cup Red Wine Vinegar
- 2 tbsp. Salt
- 1 Litre Beef Stock

Mustard Sauce

- 70g Butter
- 2 tbsp. Dijon Mustard
- 1.5 cup Heavy Cream
- 1 tbsp. Parsley finely chopped (optional)
- 1 tsp Pepper
- 1 pinch Salt

Directions

Corned Beef Method:

1. Place all ingredients into a slow cooker and cook on low for 7 hours.

Mustard Cream Method:

1. Mix the butter and mustard in a small pan over low heat
2. Add the cream and mix together. Initially the butter and the cream will stay separate but will come together as the heat rises.

3. Be very careful not to boil the sauce, as it will not combine. As the cream reduces the sauce will thicken, you want to reduce the cream by one-half.
4. Add the chopped parsley (if using), pepper and salt, and drizzle over the corned beef to serve.

Serving: 210g | Calories: 441kcal | Carbohydrates: 1g | Protein: 22.8g | Fat: 37.6g | Saturated Fat: 17.3g | Polyunsaturated Fat: 0.2g | Monounsaturated Fat: 1.2g | Trans Fat: 0.2g | Cholesterol: 93.4mg | Sodium: 1724mg | Potassium: 1.4mg | Fiber: 0g | Sugar: 1g | Vitamin A: 145IU | Vitamin C: 0mg | Calcium: 1mg | Iron: 2.1mg

CARNIVORE PIZZA CRUST

Prep time: 10 mins || Cook time: 20 mins

Serves: 6

Ingredients

Dough:

- 1¾ cup shredded mozzarella cheese
- 2 tablespoons butter or cream cheese
- ¾ cup powdered pork rinds (Pork Panko)
- 1 egg
- ⅛ teaspoon Redmond Real salt

TOPPINGS:

- Marinara Sauce (or a carnivore sauce)
- Favorite Pizza Toppings

Instructions

1. If you have a pizza stone, place it into the oven. Preheat oven to 425 degrees F.
2. To make the dough, place the mozzarella and the butter in a heat safe bowl and microwave for 1-2 minutes or until the cheese is entirely melted. Stir well.
3. Add the powered pork rinds, egg and salt and using a hand mixer, combine well.
4. Put the dough on the greased piece of parchment paper on a flat baking sheet and pat out with your hands to make a large round circle.
5. If you are using a pizza stone, transfer the pizza on the parchment and slide it onto to the hot pizza stone in the oven by sliding the parchment and pizza from the baking sheet onto the stone. Bake for 5 minutes or until the crust starts to get a little golden.
6. Remove from oven. Spread pizza sauce all over the top of the crust and mozzarella cheese and your favorite toppings.
7. Bake the pizza until the cheese is melted, about 10 minutes.
8. Store extras in an airtight container in the refrigerator for up to 3 days. Reheat slices on a baking sheet in a preheated 350°F oven for 5 minutes or until warmed through.

186 calories, 14g fat, 16g protein, 0.1g carbs, 0g fiber

BACON PIZZA

Prep time: 10 mins || Cook time: 30 mins

Serves: 4

Ingredients

- 14 slices thick cut bacon
- 6 ounces' mozzarella cheese
- ¼ cup sugar free marinara

Options:

Toppings of your choice

Instructions

1. Preheat oven to 400 degrees F.
2. Weave bacon slices together.
3. Cook for 20-25 minutes or until bacon is crisp.
4. Remove from oven and top with sauce, then cheese and toppings.
5. Return to oven and bake for 5-9 minutes (or until cheese is melted).

495 calories, 42.6g fat, 26.9g protein, 2.3g carbs, 0g fiber77% fat, 21% protein, 2% carbs

CARNIVORE WAFFLES!

These are a freaking game changer!

Recipe Makes 1 Waffle:

Ingredients:

- 2 eggs
- 1/4 cup raw breakfast sausage (this cooks in the waffle iron just fine.)
- Coconut Oil Spray (Omit if strict)

Directions

1. In a bowl crack the 2 eggs and whisk into the sausage. This will break the sausage into small bits so that it will cook evenly in the waffle iron.
2. Spray the waffle iron with Coconut Oil Spray
3. Pour the contents into the hot waffle iron and close. Let cook for approximately 3-4 minutes
4. Keep warm on a plate lined with paper towels in an oven set to 200*F
5. This is important if you are making several since they do "sweat" and can become soggy without this step.

CARNIVORE BREAKFAST SANDWICH

Prep Time: 5 Minutes || Cook Time: 5 Minutes

Servings: 1 Person

Calories: 448 Kcal

Easy, delicious, and full of protein, fats, and no plants... this breakfast sandwich is loved by those on the carnivore diet, as well as keto, or anyone who enjoys protein and fat in their diet.

While the Carnivore Breakfast Sandwich seems to be mocking the mainstream nutritional advice of avoiding cholesterol, what we really love about this breakfast sandwich is how YUMMY it is!

Ingredients

- 2 Sausage Patties beef used in picture and for calculations
- 1 egg
- 1-ounce cheddar cheese
- 1 teaspoon butter or bacon grease, if you have it

Instructions

1. In a large skillet, melt butter over medium heat. Form sausage into thin patties, about the size of your palm but only 1/2 inch thick.
2. Cook patties until they brown on one side, then flip, cooking for another 2-3 minutes, or until cooked through.
3. If you don't mind your food touching, fry an egg at the same time in the same pan. If not, you can use a little more butter in an additional pan (medium heat, and wait until the pan is hot to prevent sticking), and then assemble your carnivore breakfast sandwich.
4. Keep the yolk runny, as your sauce.
5. To assemble, place one sausage patty on a plate, then top with fried egg, slice of cheese, and another sausage patty.
6. Enjoy

Amount Per Serving (1 sandwich)

Calories 448 Calories from Fat 324 Fat 36g 55%| Cholesterol 288mg 96% |Sodium 937mg 39% | Carbohydrates 1g 0% | Protein 33g 66%

KETO STEAK NUGGETS

Ingredients

- 1 pound venison steak or beef steak, cut into chunks.
- 1 large Egg(s)
- Lard or palm oil for frying
- Keto Breading
- 1/2 cup grated parmesan cheese
- 1/2 cup pork panko
- 1/2 teaspoon Homemade Seasoned Salt

Chipotle Ranch Dip

- 1/4 cup mayonnaise
- 1/4 cup Organic Cultured Sour Cream
- 1+ teaspoon chipotle paste to taste
- 1/2 teaspoon My Ranch Dressing & Dip Mix
- 1/4 medium lime, juiced

Instructions

1. For the Chipotle Ranch Dip: Combine all ingredients, mix well. 1 teaspoon of chipotle paste yields a medium-spice version, use more or less according to your own taste preferences.
2. I encourage you to use my homemade ranch dressing and dip mix, it's superior to any store brought version. Refrigerate at least 30 minutes before serving, will keep for up to 1 week.
3. Combine Pork Panko, parmesan cheese and seasoned salt - again use my homemade not the store bought stuff. Set aside.
4. Beat 1 egg, place beaten egg 1 bowl and breading mix in another.
5. Dip chunks of steak in egg, then breading. Place on a wax paper lined sheet pan or plate.
6. FREEZE breaded raw steak bites for 30 minutes before frying. This helps to ensure that the breading will NOT LIFT when fried.
7. Heat Lard to roughly 325 degrees F. Working in batches as necessary, fry steak nuggets (from frozen or chilled) until browned, about 2-3 minutes.
8. Transfer to a paper towel lined plate, season with a sprinkle of salt and serve with Chipotle Ranch.

Notes

I make several batches of Keto Steak Bites and store them raw, in the freezer for up to 6 months. They can be frozen solid and fried.

Nutrition

Calories: 350kcal | Carbohydrates: 1g | Protein: 40g | Fat: 20g | Saturated Fat: 6g | Cholesterol: 163mg | Sodium: 335mg | Potassium: 491mg | Sugar: 1g | Vitamin A: 220IU | Calcium: 100mg | Iron: 5mg

MAIN DISHES

KETO TACO PIE

Prep Time: 20 minutes || Cook Time: 30 minutes

Servings: 8 people

Calories: 353kcal

Serving Size: 100 grams = 3.5 Ounce Slice

This is an easy and delicious recipe, great for a quick family friendly weeknight meal. You can whip this dish up in probably less than 1 hour. With only 4 ingredients it is sure to hit the spot.

Ingredients

- 1 lb. Ground Beef
- 3 tbsp. Taco Seasoning
- 6 Eggs
- 1 cup Heavy Cream
- 1 cup Cheese Shredded

Instructions

1. In a skillet, brown your ground beef.
2. Season with taco seasoning
3. Preheat oven to 350 degrees. Using a blender or by hand combine the eggs, cream, and season if desired. Mix well.
4. Place your cooked and seasoned ground beef in your pie pan. Sprinkle with half of your shredded cheese (reserve some for later)

5. Slow pour your cream mixture over your ground beef and cheese. Sprinkle remaining cheese on top.
6. Bake for 30 minutes or until the center is set and the cheese browned. Remove from oven and let sit for 5-10 minutes.

Enjoy!

Net Carbs; 1 Gram per slice

Serving: 100g | Calories: 353kcal | Carbohydrates: 2g | Protein: 18g | Fat: 30g | Saturated Fat: 15g | Cholesterol: 219mg | Sodium: 264mg | Potassium: 235mg | Fiber: 1g | Sugar: 1g | Vitamin A: 850IU | Vitamin C: 0.7mg | Calcium: 150mg | Iron: 1.8mg

KETO-CARNIVORE BLACK PUDDING

These black puddings are made from meat, fat and blood only and contain no fillers – a carnivorous delight! They freeze very well and do not keep for long in the fridge, so making small puddings is preferable.

I added liver and pig skin so that there is the advantage of some offal and collagen in these puddings which, for those not too keen on liver, is a great way to incorporate it as you really cannot tell it is even in there!

Ingredients & Equipment:

- 500g ground pork shoulder
- 50g lamb liver – minced
- 50g pig skin – minced
- 250g pork back fat – diced
- 150g dried pigs blood
- 600ml water – warm
- 6tsp sea salt
- Ox middles/bungs (these are large, edible and strong sausage casings)
- Short cable tie wraps
- 2 Funnels or 2 sausage making tubes (one larger than the other)
- An apron – just in case you spill or splash any of the blood!

Directions:

To prepare the pig skin:

1. Place in a large pan of boiling water and simmer for a couple of hours until soft.

2. Allow to cool and then place in a food processor to mince.
3. Set aside.

To prepare the liver:

1. Place in a food processor and mince.
2. Set aside.
3. To prepare the pork shoulder:
4. Either buy ground or cut into cubes and grind yourself with an electric grinder using the large grinding blade – make sure the meat is very cold as this will make it easier to grind.
5. Set aside.

To prepare the back fat:

1. Slice the fat into strips and then dice into small pieces.
2. Set aside.

To prepare the blood:

1. Measure 150g into a large jug and pour in 600ml of warm water and whisk until smooth.
2. Set aside.

To prepare the ox middles/bungs:

1. Soak in cold water for at least 20 minutes prior to use.

Making The Puddings:

2. Place all the pre-prepared meat ingredients into a large bowl and mix together.
3. Slowly add the rehydrated blood, mixing in thoroughly. (Be careful not to splash it about or you will look like you are on a horror movie set!!)
4. Add the salt and mix in.
5. Place another clean bowl next to your large bowl.
6. Roll the ox middles onto the funnel/largest sausage tube.
7. Use a cable tie wrap to close the end tightly.
8. Using a large serving spoon, start to carefully spoon the mixture into the funnel/tube and use the smaller sausage tube to push it down into the ox middle.
9. Use your other hand to guide the mixture into the ox middle, making sure there are no gaps or air pockets, feeding the pudding into the clean bowl.
10. Make sure that there is enough of the liquid blood being added along with the meats.
11. Do not make each pudding too long before using another cable tie to close it off tightly, making sure that the pudding is firmly packed.

12. Leave a small gap in the ox middle (where you will later cut it) and then close off another section to start a new pudding.
13. Continue until all the mixture has been used.
14. Securely tie the last pudding and then cut each pudding between the cable ties to separate. Bring a large pan of water to the boil.
15. Place the individual puddings into the water, turn down the heat and simmer for between an hour to an hour and a half.
16. Remove the puddings from the hot water and place immediately into a bowl of ice water and leave to cool.
17. Place into a dish and into the fridge overnight.
18. ENJOY!

INSTANT POT STEAK SOUP

I've been making this regularly since starting the diet and certainly consider it one of my "must have" recipes as far as keeping things interesting on a way of eating as strict as the carnivore diet, which for most people is just meat, salt and water.

Ingredients:

- Leftover steak and bones, could also be fresh steak and bones with no issues.
- Salt
- Water
- ½ giant clove of garlic (or two regular sized cloves)
- Salt, I like to use a blend because they do taste different and add different flavor profiles without adding carbs
- Pepper
- Balsamic Vinegar (Optional According to some, others claim it's necessary to pull all nutrients out of the bones)
- Worsteshire sauce (necessary for delicious flavors)
- Water

Directions

1. Put everything above in the instant pot in no particular order, the spices and sauces to taste.
2. I add enough water to cover the meat which leaves me with moist meat and bone broth out of it.

3. Set the instant pot on the meat/stew option for at least two hours, up to four hours. Make sure the valve is set to close.
4. Instant release when the timer goes off.
5. Lots of stirring and sometimes a bit of boiling does the recipe well, generally due to lack of agitation in the pot when you open it everything will be in separate layers and it likely won't look very good.
6. I also generally use a fork to smash down larger fat pieces, once they're in pea size pieces you don't notice the texture when eating.
7. Salt and serve immediately. It does store, just refrigerate and reheat with a bit of water. Do not be surprised when it turns to meat jello in the fridge, that means you did it right.
8. Can also be frozen until later but I generally make enough for a few days at a time and eat a lot of it.

EASY OSSO BUCCO

Ingredients

- 3-5 pounds of shank from pork, beef, or wild game
- 2 tbsp. fat of choice (i.e. tallow, bacon fat, butter, olive oil, etc)
- 2-4 cups chopped vegetables of choice (optional)
- 2 tbsp. apple cider vinegar
- salt & pepper
- 1-quart bone broth or stock of choice

Instructions

1. Preheat oven to 325 F
2. In an oven-proof pot, such as a Dutch oven, melt the fat of choice over medium heat
3. Sear all sides of the meat, about 1-2 minutes each side, then set aside
4. In the same pot, add the chopped vegetables if using. Sauté for about 10 minutes
5. Add the apple cider vinegar, allow to cook a couple of minutes more
6. Then add the bone broth
7. Place the seared meat on top of the vegetables, season with salt and pepper.
8. Cover and transfer to oven, cook for 3 hours
9. Optional: baste meat with pan juices hourly. This isn't necessary but I find it makes the meat more juicy
10. Serve along with juices from the pot

Notes

If adding vegetables, make sure to use dense ones that can withstand long cooking times, like cauliflower, onions, cabbage, turnip, rutabaga, beets, etc.

PRESSURE COOKER PORK LOIN ROAST

Prep Time: 10 mins || Cook Time: 35 mins

Course: Main Course

Servings: 9 people

Calories: 220kcal

Pressuring cooking a pork loin roast results in tender and juicy meat every time. And it's a faster cooking method than using the oven or slow cooker.

Ingredients

- 3 pounds pork loin roast
- 1 teaspoon onion powder
- 1 teaspoon dried oregano
- 1 teaspoon garlic powder
- 1 teaspoon ground cumin
- 1 teaspoon dried thyme
- 1 teaspoon coriander
- 1/2 teaspoon kosher salt or more if desired
- 1 tablespoon oil
- 2 cloves garlic minced
- 2 cups chicken bone broth

Instructions

1. Mix onion powder, oregano, garlic powder, cumin, thyme, coriander, and salt in a small bowl. Rub seasoning mix into pork loin roast.
2. Heat oil in pressure cooker on sauté then stir fry minced garlic until fragrant. Add pork loin roast and brown all sides.
3. Remove roast and deglaze pot with half the bone broth.
4. Add remaining broth then place rack in bottom of pot. Put the pork loin roast on top of the rack.
5. Pressure cook on high for 25 minutes. When done, do a quick pressure release. Remove roast from pot and allow to sit for 10-15 before slicing.

Serving: 151grams | Calories: 220kcal | Carbohydrates: 1g | Protein: 34g | Fat: 7g | Saturated Fat: 2g | Cholesterol: 95mg | Sodium: 266mg | Potassium: 615mg | Fiber: 0g | Sugar: 0g | Vitamin C: 3.9mg | Calcium: 20mg | Iron: 1.3mg

BRAISED BEEF HEART WITH BONE MARROW

Prep Time: 15 minutes || Cook Time: 6 hours

Category: Heart, Organ meat

Servings: 8

Ingredients

- 2lb beef heart, trimmed
- salt
- 1-4 marrow bones
- 8 sprigs thyme
- 2 sprigs rosemary
- 2 bay leaves

Instructions

1. Trim beef heart of any connective tissue and season well with salt a day in advance.
2. Add heart to dutch oven, along with marrow bones and thyme, rosemary and bay leaves. Add water to cover.
3. Cook on 290F for six hours. Optionally add vegetables of choice and check meat stock for seasoning 50 minutes before dinner.
4. Slice heart lengthwise, spoon marrow over the top, and serve with stock.

EASY HOMEMADE JERKY FROM GROUND BEEF

Prep Time: 20 Minutes Cook Time: 12 Hours

Servings: 20 Sticks

Calories: 115 Kcal

Beef jerky is an easy portable way to get needed protein in either as a quick snack, or even a meal replacement in a pinch. I love to bring this camping and when we do errands or otherwise are out and about. Less chewy than beef jerky from a roast, this beef jerky from ground beef is crunchy if you roll it out thinly.

Ingredients

- 2 pounds ground beef
- 2 tablespoons sea salt
- 1 teaspoon ground black pepper
- 1 teaspoon other spices as desired (I like garlic powder and smoked paprika, 1 teaspoon each)
- Equipment needed: Dehydrator optional paraflex sheets, optional jerky gun

Instructions

1. In a bowl, mix seasonings into the beef until evenly distributed, with your hands. Divide beef mixture into 3 or 4 sections.
2. Roll to the size of your dehydrator trays between either paraflex sheets or plastic wrap if you don't have paraflex sheets.
3. Remove plastic wrap as you flip the meat onto the dehydrator trays. Score into jerky-sized strips with a sharp knife, being careful not to cut the dehydrator tray, and dry on high overnight, or until thoroughly cooked. Break apart at the score lines.
4. Store in the fridge long term, though the salt and dehydrator preserve this well to last for a weekend camping trip or all day on a hike.

RECIPE NOTES

Tip: Use scissors, like the ones that came with your knife set, to easily cut this jerky once dehydrated.

Tip 2: You can also use a jerky gun to make thin even strips of jerky without having to roll it out. This is a great job for older kids (it's a little hard for toddlers) and I think it's fun too!

Amount Per Serving (1 piece)

Calories 115Calories from Fat 81, Fat 9g14%, Saturated Fat 3g 15%, Cholesterol 32mg 11%, Sodium 728mg 30%, Potassium 122mg 3%, Protein 7g 14%, Calcium 8mg 1%, Iron 0.9mg 5%

HARDCORE CARNIVORE BLACK SMOKED BEEF RIBS

One of the hallmarks of Texas barbecue - impossibly tender beef with a killer crust thanks to our Black seasoning.

Ingredients:

- One section of beef plate ribs (3 ribs total, about 4-5 lb.)
- 3-4 tablespoons Hardcore Carnivore Black rub
- 1/4 cup vinegar (white or cider)
- 3/4 cup water

Directions:

1. Preheat a smoker to 300f.
2. Prepare beef ribs. Leave the membrane on the bones intact. Pat dry with paper towel. Apply the Hardcore Carnivore Black rub. Be generous with your application, more is better. Coat all sides and massage it in well.

3. Place the rack of ribs in the smoker, bone side down. In a spray bottle, combine the water and vinegar. After 2 hours, spritz with the vinegar mixture every hour or so.
4. Cook until a probe or skewer has no resistance when pushed in. This will be at about 206-210f. Make sure you probe the rack in several spots. It should feel just like a hot knife through butter - if you feel any kind of resistance, they are not done yet.
5. Once cooked, remove rack and wrap in Hardcore Carnivore butchers paper, then set in a cooler to rest for 1-3 hours. If you cannot get paper you can use foil, but your bark will soften. Slice ribs between bone and serve.

KETO SMOKEY BACON MEATBALLS RECIPE

Prep Time: 15 minutes || Cook Time: 30 minutes

Yield: 8 servings

Category: Dinner

These Keto meatballs smoke the competition.

Ingredients

- 2 chicken breasts or 1 lb. (450 g) ground chicken
- 8 slices of bacon, cooked and crumbled
- 1 egg, whisked
- 2 cloves of garlic, peeled
- 1 Tablespoon (7 g) onion powder
- 2 drops of liquid smoke
- 4 Tablespoons (60 ml) olive oil, to cook with

Instructions

1. Place everything (except the oil) into a food processor and mix well.
2. From the mixture, form 20-24 small meatballs.
3. Place the oil into a large frying pan, and fry the meatballs until the meat is cooked (cook one side for 5 minutes until browned, then flip and cook the other side for 5-10 minutes until done). You will probably need to cook them in a few batches.

Net Carbs: 1 g, Calories: 280 Sugar: 0 g Fat: 25 g Carbohydrates: 1 g Fiber: 0 g Protein: 13 g

PORK BELLY BACON BURNT ENDS

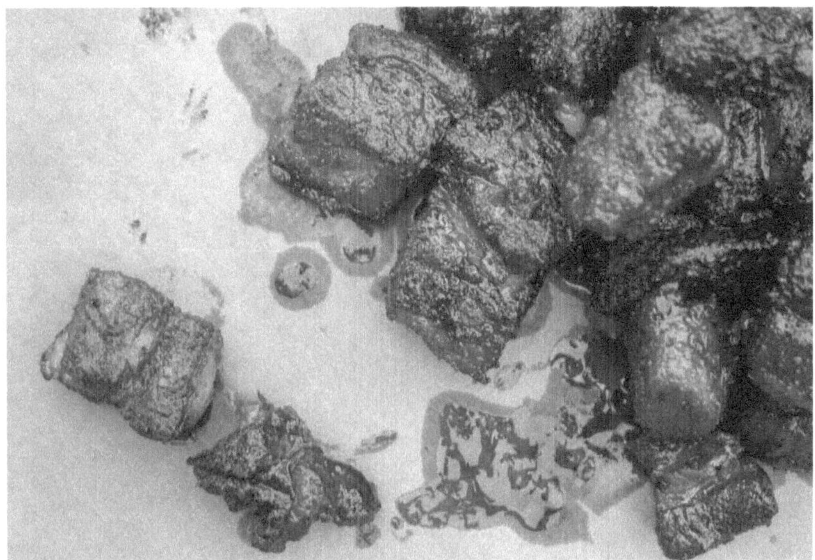

Get ready for legit pork candy with these smokey, sweet and saucy pork belly burnt ends.

Ingredients:

- 4-5 lb. pork belly
- 6 tablespoons Hardcore Carnivore Red seasoning
- 1 cup BBQ sauce (we like Meat Mitch Whomp)
- 3 tablespoons honey
- 3 tablespoons butter, cut into chunks.

Directions

1. Heat a smoker to 250f.
2. Cut belly into 1.5 inch cubes, and season liberally with Hardcore Carnivore red, making sure all sides are coated.
3. Place the belly cubes onto a wire rack, and place this into the smoker. Cook for two hours.
4. Remove cubes from rack and place into a large foil pan - large enough so that they are spread out in a single layer. Pour over BBQ sauce and honey, and stir so cubes are coated. Dot butter over the top of the pork then cover the pan with foil and return to smoker for another 1.5 hours.
5. Remove the foil, and allow the cubes to cook a further 30 minutes, so sauce can thicken and caramelize.

KETO CARNIVORE CHICKEN ENCHILADAS

Prep Time: 15 Minutes || Cook Time: 15 Minutes

Serving Size: 1

Yield: 10

Use your favorite keto friendly ingredients in these delicious chicken enchiladas.

Ingredients

- 2 boneless skinless chicken breasts
- 1 teaspoon dried garlic
- juice of 1 lime or 3 tablespoons bottled lime juice
- Chimichurri sauce or 1 bunch of cilantro, pureed with 1 tablespoon olive oil
- 16 ounce package of sliced chicken or turkey sandwich meat
- 8 ounces shredded cheese
- 8 ounces of spinach, cooked
- 1 bell pepper sliced
- 1 jar of salsa verde or enchilada sauce

Instructions

TO MAKE THE SHREDDED CHICKEN:

1. Place the chicken breasts in a crockpot and drizzle the lime juice over them.
2. Top with the chimichurri sauce. If you don't have chimichurri sauce made (or store bought) then you can make your own cilantro sauce by placing the leaves from a bunch of cilantro in the blender or food processor, adding a tablespoon of olive oil and blending until it pureed.
3. Sprinkle the garlic over the chicken.
4. Cook the chicken on low for 8 hours or high for 4-5.
5. Once the chicken is cooked remove it from the crockpot and use two forks to shred the chicken.

TO ASSEMBLE THE ENCHILADAS:

1. Preheat the oven to 400F.
2. Prep the other ingredients. Slice the pepper thinly. Cook the spinach until it is soft and squeeze out the excess water. Plan to use only half the cheese inside of the enchiladas.
3. Using four slices of the chicken/turkey sandwich meat to create the enchilada wrapper start by placing two slices down next to each other slightly over lapping. Add two more next to those making sure they also slightly over lap.
4. Make a small row of shredded chicken in the middle of the sandwich meat wrapper.
5. On the side closest to you, add a row of each of the other ingredients... spinach, a few pepper strips and some cheese.
6. Begin to roll the enchilada by pulling the slices of sandwich meat across the top of the filling and gently squeezing them to one side. Roll the enchilada away from you but continue to squeeze the rolled fillings toward you to keep them tightly wrapped. Keep in mind that the sliced sandwich meat isn't as firm as a flour based tortilla wrapper.
7. Continue to roll up and, once completely rolled, place seem side down in a pan.
8. Continue to prepare all the enchiladas. Once they are all in the pan spoon two tablespoons of salsa verde or enchilada sauce over them.
9. Sprinkle the half of the cheese that had been reserved.
10. Place in the oven and bake for 12 to 15 minutes or until the cheese is melted.
11. Remove from oven and serve.

Calories 271, Total Fat 7g, Sodium 411mg, Carbohydrates 8g, Net Carbohydrates 6g, Fiber 2g, Protein 25g

CARNIVORE RISOTTO

Cook Time: 1 hour

Servings: 2

Ingredients

- 1 chorizo sausage
- 1/2 roasted potato
- 1/2 orange pepper
- 1/2 yellow pepper
- 1/2 green pepper
- 1/2 cup green beans
- 1/2 can sweetcorn
- 1 cup risotto rice
- 1/2 cup lardons
- 1 tbsp. olive oil
- 2 clove garlic
- 1 can tomatoes
- water

Directions

1. Bring oven to temperature and roast the potato for 25 minutes
2. Slice chorizo into 1 cm thick pieces and fry in a large pan in olive oil
3. Add in lardons when mostly done, and then garlic

4. Add in the peppers and fry until softened. Then the green beans and sweetcorn
5. Slice potato into cubes and add this, too. Fry until coated in oil
6. Add a can of chopped tomatoes, then fill half of it with water and add this too
7. Add the rice. Stir in well, then cover the pan and let it sit for 20 minutes, or until the rice has absorbed all the water. DO NOT STIR WHILST COOKING!!!

SIMPLIFIED CARNIVORE ALA DREW

Ingredients

- Beef (Sirloin)
- Salmon
- Salt
- Egg Recipe
- 2-3 eggs
- Butter or cream

Directions

1. Place Beef and Salmon on a baking tray. Feel free to sprinkle a liberal amount of salt to taste. (Salt is a very important mineral for the carnivore diet)
2. Grill at 180 Celsius for about 8 minutes.
3. Mix the eggs with butter in a bowl (or cream)
4. Microwave 'egg recipe' for 2 mins.
5. Once done, transfer everything on a plate and enjoy.

ONE-SKILLET TUCAN PORK CHOPS

Prep Time: 5 minutes||Cook Time: 25 minutes

Course: Main Course

Servings: 4

Calories: 856kcal

A fast and flavorful one-pan meal with pork chops and smothered in a creamy sauce is a perfect weeknight recipe ready in 35 minutes!

EQUIPMENT

10-12″ Cast Iron Skillet or other oven safe skillet

Ingredients

For the Chops

- 2 tbsp. butter or oil divided
- 1.5 – 2 lbs bone-in pork chops
- Salt and pepper

For the Sauce:

- ½ Onion
- 4 cloves Garlic
- ¼ cup Roasted Red Peppers
- 4 cups Spinach
- 1 14 oz jar Cannellini beans drained and rinsed
- 1 cup Heavy Cream
- For Garnish
- Tomatoes
- Parsley
- Salt
- Pepper

Instructions

1. Prep the oven:
2. Preheat the oven to 375 degrees F.
3. Sear the chops:
4. Melt 1 tablespoon of the butter in a skillet pre-heated oven medium-high heat.
5. Pat the pork chops dry and season with salt and pepper.

6. Sear the pork chops in the skillet on each side 2 to 5 minutes, until a golden crust forms. If the chop does not easily pull from the pan, the crust has not formed yet. The pork will release easily when the crust has formed. Pulling too soon can cause tearing.
7. Remove the chops, cover and set aside.

Saute the Veggies:

1. In the same pan, melt the remaining butter and add sautee the onion until soft, 5 minutes. Add the garlic and cook 30 seconds longer.
2. Mix in the roasted red pepper and toss to combine.
3. Add the spinach. It will overflow the pan and look like too much, but as you stir and the spinach wilts it withers to a minimal portion.
4. Toss in the beans.

Make the Sauce:

1. Off heat, slowly whisk in the cream, scraping up any browned bits as you do so.
2. Finish Cooking the Chops:
3. Nestle the chops back into the pan.
4. Sprinkle fontina cheese over the dish and slide in the oven to cook.
5. Cook until the chops read 145 degrees F with an instant-read thermometer, about 5 to 7 minutes longer.

Serve:

1. Serve the chops by arranging on a platter over pasta. Spoon the sauce over the pasta.
2. Garnish with chopped tomatoes, minced parsley and salt and pepper, if desired.

NOTES

The thickness of your chops will greatly change the cook time. This recipe was made with 1" bone-in chops. Pork chops should be cooked to an internal temperature of 145 degrees.

Substitutions:

- Fresh rosemary goes great in this dish and I love adding a sprig or two if I have some on hand. I will also mince some fresh rosemary and toss it in with the cream as it simmers.
- If you don't have white cannellini beans, swap in chickpeas.
- Swap Parmesan for the Fontina if you don't have any on hand

CARNIVORE DOG

Prep Time: 5 minutes || Cook Time: 20 minutes

Serves: 8 People

Ingredients

- 8 Oz H-E-B Fully Cooked Seasoned Pork Carnitas
- 4 slices of bacon
- 8 H-E-B Texas Heritage Beef Hot Dogs
- 10 Oz H-E-B Coleslaw Kit, prepared according to package instructions
- 2 Tbsp H-E-B That Green Sauce
- 8 hot dog buns, warmed

Instructions

1. In a large sauté pan over medium-high heat, cook pork carnitas until crispy and heated through.
2. If pork sticks, add about a teaspoon of oil. Remove pork from pan and keep warm.
3. In same pan, cook bacon over same heat until crispy, about 8 to 10 minutes.
4. Remove bacon and drain grease on paper towels. Once cool enough to handle, crumbled bacon.
5. Cook hot dogs in bacon grease, rotating with tongs until entire dog is browned and crispy, about 5 minutes.
6. Add green sauce to prepared coleslaw. Combine well.
7. To prepare dog, place hot dog in bun and top with a spoonful of pork, coleslaw and bacon crumbles.

Chef's Note: Serve dog with chips and queso or your favorite tailgating sides.

Serving Size 130g

Calories 270 Calories From Fat 200 Total Fat 23g 35%, Saturated Fat 9g 45%, Trans Fat 0.5g, Cholesterol 55 mg 18%, Sodium 690 mg 29%, Total Carbohydrate 5g 2%, Dietary Fiber 1g 4%, Sugars 2g, Protein 12g

TRIPLE MEAT KETO CARNIVORE CHILI

Prep Time: 5 mins || Cook Time: 8 hrs.

Course: Main Course, Soup

Servings: 20 cups

Calories: 172 kcal

Three types of meat make this Keto Carnivore chili extra delicious by incorporating different textures.

Ingredients

- 2 cups onion chopped
- 3 cloves garlic minced
- 64 ounces diced tomatoes
- 32 ounces crushed tomatoes
- 2 tablespoons jalapeno chopped
- 1 tablespoon chili powder
- 5 tablespoon spicy chili powder
- 5 teaspoon black pepper

- 2 teaspoons salt
- 1 teaspoon molasses
- 1 bottle corona premier beer
- 1 pound beef short ribs
- 1 pound ground beef
- 1 pound beef chuck diced

Toppings

- shredded cheese

Instructions

1. Add all ingredients except the meat to the crockpot.
2. Stir to combine and taste to adjust spices to your liking.
3. Add all meat and stir to combine.
4. Cook on low for 9 hours or on high for 6 hours.
5. Take out the short ribs and remove meat from bone.
6. Dice short rib meat and mix back into chili.
7. Serve with cheese or whatever other toppings you like.

Recipe Notes

For a spicier version of this chili, replace the regular chili powder with all hot chili powder and add 1 tablespoon of chopped habanero, about 1 pepper. Add 2 tablespoons chipotle in adobo sauce and 2 chopped chipotle peppers.

Calories 172Calories from Fat 81, Fat 9g 14%, Saturated Fat 3g 19%, Cholesterol 41mg 14%, Sodium 357mg 16%, Potassium 548mg 16%, Carbohydrates 9g 3%, Fiber 2g 8%, Sugar 5g 6%, Protein 13g 26%, Vitamin A 400IU 8%, Vitamin C 15.7mg 19%, Calcium 61mg 6%, Iron 2.9mg 16%

WAXMAN'S BRISKET OF BEEF

Prep Time: 7 Minutes||Cook Time: 4 Hours

Serves: 10 To 12

Ingredients

- 1 6-pound first-cut (a.k.a. flat-cut) beef brisket, trimmed so that a thin layer of fat remains
- 2 teaspoons all-purpose flour (or matzoh meal)
- 1 pinch Freshly ground black pepper
- 3 tablespoons corn oil (or other neutral oil)
- 8 medium onions, peeled and thickly sliced
- 3 tablespoons tomato paste
- 1 pinch Kosher salt
- 3 cloves garlic
- 1 carrot, peeled

Directions

1. Heat the oven to 350°F.
2. Lightly dust the brisket with flour, then sprinkle with pepper to taste. Heat the oil over medium-high heat in a large ovenproof enameled cast-iron pot or other heavy pot with a lid just large enough to hold the brisket snugly.
3. Add the brisket to the pot and brown on both sides until crusty brown areas appear on the surface here and there, 5 to 7 minutes per side.
4. Transfer the brisket to a platter, turn up the heat a bit, then add the onions to the pot and stir constantly with a wooden spoon, scraping up any browned bits stuck to the bottom of the pot.
5. Cook until the onions have softened and developed a rich brown color but aren't yet caramelized, 10 to 15 minutes.
6. Turn off the heat and place the brisket and any accumulated juices on top of the onions.
7. Spread the tomato paste over the brisket as if you were icing a cake. Sprinkle with salt and more pepper to taste, then add the garlic and carrot to the pot. Cover the pot, transfer to the oven, and cook the brisket for 1 1/2 hours.
8. Transfer the brisket to a cutting board and, using a very sharp knife, slice the meat across the grain into approximately 1/8-inch-thick slices.
9. Return the slices to the pot, overlapping them at an angle so that you can see a bit of the top edge of each slice. The end result should resemble the original unsliced brisket leaning slightly backward. Check the seasonings and, if the sauce appears dry, add 2 to 3 teaspoons of water to the pot.

10. Cover the pot and return to the oven. Lower the heat to 325°F and cook the brisket until it is fork-tender, 1 1/2 to 2 hours. Check once or twice during cooking to make sure that the liquid is not bubbling away. If it is, add a few more teaspoons of water—but not more. Also, each time you check, spoon some of the liquid on top of the roast so that it drips down between the slices.
11. It is ready to serve with its juices, but, in fact, it's even better the second day. It also freezes well.

OLIVE OIL-BASTED GRASS-FED STRIP STEAK

Total Time: 25 Mins

Yield: Serves 4 (serving size: about 3 oz.)

Ingredients

- 3 tablespoons olive oil, divided
- 2 (8-oz.) 1 1/2-in.-thick grass-fed New York strip steaks, trimmed
- 1 teaspoon kosher salt, divided
- 1 teaspoon freshly ground black pepper, divided
- 1 (3-in.) rosemary sprig
- 1 garlic clove, crushed
- Rosemary leaves (optional)

Directions

1. Heat grill pan over medium-high. Brush 1 tablespoon oil on steaks; sprinkle with 1/2 teaspoon each salt and pepper.
2. Add rosemary sprig, garlic, and 1 tablespoon oil to pan. Add steaks; cook 9 minutes or until desired degree of doneness, turning steaks and basting with oil once every minute.
3. Place steaks on a cutting board; let stand 5 minutes. Slice steaks across grain; place on a platter. Drizzle with juices from cutting board and remaining 1 tablespoon oil. Sprinkle with remaining 1/2 teaspoon each salt and pepper. Garnish with rosemary leaves, if desired.

Calories 224 Fat 13.2g Satfat 2.6g Monofat 8.5g Polyfat 1.2g Protein 26g Carbohydrate 0.0g Fiber 0.0g Cholesterol 62mg Iron 2mg Sodium 543mg Calcium 13mg Sugars 0g Est. added sugars 0g

GRILLED SPLIT LOBSTER

Servings: 2

Cooking lobster entirely on the grill ensures that no water gets inside the shell, which means you'll get more concentrated lobster flavor.

Ingredients

- 2 tablespoons vegetable oil, plus more for grill
- 2 1½-pound live lobsters
- Kosher salt and freshly ground black pepper
- Melted unsalted butter, hot sauce, and lemon wedges (for serving)

Directions

1. Prepare grill for medium-high heat; oil grate. Chill lobsters in freezer 15 minutes (this will slow down their nervous system—helpful for what comes next).
2. Working one at a time, transfer to a cutting board, belly side down, with head facing you. Using a kitchen towel, hold tail (it shouldn't be very active now) and, starting where the tail meets the body, bisect body and head lengthwise in one fell swoop.
3. Turn lobster around and cut lengthwise through tail. Remove any tomalley or eggs (reserving, if you'd like).

4. Immediately rub cut side of lobsters with 2 Tbsp. oil total; season with salt and pepper. Grill, cut side down, pressing claws against grill, until meat is nearly cooked through, 6–8 minutes.
5. Turn and grill until shells are lightly charred and meat is cooked through (tail meat will look opaque and be firm), about 3 minutes. Remove lobsters from grill and serve with butter, hot sauce, and lemon wedges for squeezing over.

Calories (kcal) 290 Fat (g) 16 Saturated Fat (g) 2.5 Cholesterol (mg) 280 Carbohydrates (g) 0 Dietary Fiber (g) 0 Total Sugars (g) 0 Protein (g) 36 Sodium (mg) 930

DUCK LEG CONFIT

Time: Overnight + 2.5 hours of cooking

Servings: 4

Ingredients

- 4 duck leg portions with thighs attached, excess fat trimmed and reserved
- 1 tablespoon plus 1/8 teaspoon kosher salt
- 1/2 teaspoon freshly ground black pepper
- 10 garlic cloves
- 4 bay leaves
- 4 sprigs fresh thyme
- 1 1/2 teaspoons black peppercorns
- 1/2 teaspoon table salt
- 4 cups olive oil or duck fat

Directions

1. Lay the leg portions on a platter, skin side down. Sprinkle with 1 tablespoon of the kosher salt and black pepper.
2. Place the garlic cloves, bay leaves, and sprigs of thyme on each of 2 leg portions. Lay the remaining 2 leg portions, flesh to flesh, on top. put the reserved fat from the ducks in the bottom of a glass or plastic container.
3. Top with the sandwiched leg portions. Sprinkle with the remaining 1/8 teaspoon kosher salt. Cover and refrigerate for 12 hours.
4. Preheat the oven to 300 degrees F.
5. Remove the duck from the refrigerator. Remove the garlic, bay leaves, thyme, and duck fat and reserve. Rinse the duck with cool water, rubbing off some of the salt and pepper. Pat dry with paper towels.
6. Put the reserved garlic, bay leaves, thyme, and duck fat in the bottom of an enameled cast-iron pot. Sprinkle evenly with the peppercorns and salt. Lay the duck on top, skin side down. Add the olive oil/duck fat. Cover and bake for 2.5 to 3 hours, or until the meat pulls away from the bone.
7. Remove the duck from the fat. Strain the fat and reserve.
8. To serve immediately, sear duck legs skin-side down in a hot pan until the skin is golden and crispy (about 3-4 minutes) or to save for later: pick the meat from the bones and place it in a stoneware container.
9. Cover the meat with some of the strained fat, making a 1/4-inch layer. The duck confit can be stored in the refrigerator for up to one month.

KETOGENIC GRILLED BEEF LIVER

Prep Time: 10 minutes || Cook Time: 7 minutes

Servings: 5

Calories: 315kcal

Course: Dinner, Lunch

This grilled beef liver is so delicious. If you love organ meat, you must give this a try!

Ingredients

- 1 lb. beef liver cut into thin slices
- ½ cup olive oil
- 1 clove garlic crushed
- 1 tbsp. fresh mint finely chopped
- 1 tsp salt
- ¼ tsp black pepper freshly ground

Instructions

1. Preheat a large grill pan over medium-high heat.
2. Rinse the liver thoroughly under cold running water. Make sure to wash out all the blood traces. Pat dry with a paper towel. Using a sharp knife, remove all tough veins, if any. Cut crosswise into thin slices.
3. In a small bowl, combine olive oil with crushed garlic, mint, salt, and pepper. Mix until well incorporated. Generously brush the liver slices with this mixture and grill for 5-7 minutes on each side. Enjoy!

Calories 315Calories from Fat 225, Fat 25g38%, Saturated Fat 4g20%, Cholesterol 249mg83%, Sodium 528mg22%, Potassium 284mg8%, Carbohydrates 4g1%, Sugar 1g1%, Protein 19g38%, Vitamin A 15345IU307%, Vitamin C 1.4mg2%, Calcium 5mg1%, Iron 4.6mg26%

SLOW SMOKED PORK AND BEANS

Prep Time: 10 minutes || Cook Time: 3 hours10 minutes

Course: Side Dish

Calories: 238kcal

Servings: 8

Every family has their version of pork and beans. Usually something a little tinkered with by mom or dad, then tinkered with some more when you start dabbling in your own kitchen. This is a basic version of that. Adjust it to your families traditions and tastebuds.

EQUIPMENT

Smoker

Aluminum tin / pan

Ingredients

- 1 16 oz can pork and beans
- 1 cup leftover shredded pork
- 1/2 onion minced
- 1/4 cup maple syrup
- 1/4 cup brown sugar
- 1/2 cup ketchup
- 1 tbs dijon mustard
- 4 strips bacon cooked and chopped

Instructions

1. Prep your wood and smoker for 225 degrees and get things going.
2. Mix the pork and beans in an 8×8 aluminium pan with the pork, onion, maple syrup, brown sugar, ketchup, mustard and bacon.
3. Place in the smoker for 2 to 3 hours, until bubbling and hot through.
4. Remove, cover with foil and let cool 5 to 10 minutes before serving.
5. Spoon out deliciousness.

NOTES

This recipe is a great base recipe. See my notes above on other additions you can mix in to create your own unique flavors.

Another great way to mix up the flavor here is to get several smaller cans of different versions of baked beans and letting their flavors mingle while they smoke.

PHILLY CHEESESTEAK FRIES

Prep Time: 5 Minutes || Cook Time: 35 Minutes

Yield: 1 Platter

Go big with your next home tailgating party with a giant platter of these loaded Philly cheesesteak fries! Fresh steak, peppers, onions slathered in cheese over scoop-able fries - heck yeah!

Ingredients

- 1 24oz package frozen waffle fries
- 8 oz rib eye steak
- salt
- ½ green bell pepper, seeded and sliced thin
- ½ onion, sliced thin
- 2 tbsp. Worcestershire sauce
- 8 oz provolone cheese, shredded
- Ground black pepper
- Mayo, Ketchup or other desired condiments

Instructions

1. Preheat oven as instructed for the fries.
2. Arrange two baking sheets and divide the fries equally between the two in a single layer. Bake until golden brown and cooked through.
3. Meanwhile, season the steak liberally with salt.
4. Preheat a heavy-duty cast-iron skillet, to medium heat.
5. Cook the steak, 2 to 3 minutes a side, until a great crust forms and it pulls back without any resistance.
6. Remove the steak and wrap in foil.
7. In the same skillet, toss in the peppers and onions. Allow to caramelize for 3 to 5 minutes.
8. Add the Worcestershire sauce, black pepper, and cover. Cook until tender, about 5 minutes longer.
9. Slice the steak into paper thin strips. Remove the fries from the oven and set to broil.
10. Arrange a layer of fries on the pan, top with ¼ of the cheese, 1/4 steak, peppers and onions. Set under the broiler for 1 minute just to melt the cheese.
11. Carefully remove and pile the rest of the fries on top. Cover in the remaining peppers, onions, steak and cheese.
12. Place under the broiler one more time for 2 to 3 minutes, until the cheese has melted.

13. Remove and allow the pan to cool to the touch placing safely but allowing guests to serve themselves from the warm platter of cheesy fries.

Amount Per Serving: Calories: 480 Total Fat: 25g Saturated Fat: 10g Trans Fat: 0g, Unsaturated Fat: 14g, Cholesterol: 64mg, Sodium: 938mg, Carbohydrates: 43g, Fiber: 2g, Sugar: 4g, Protein: 21g

MEDITERRANEAN GRILLED CHICKEN SALAD

Prep Time: 10 minutes || Cook Time: 10 minutes

Servings: 4 servings

Calories: 2619kcal

Course: Salad

Ingredients

- 3 lbs boneless skinless chicken breasts
- 1 package Wild Garden Persian Marinade
- 3 lemons divided
- 1/2 red onion sliced
- 1 red pepper stem and seeds removed, chopped
- 1 orange pepper stem and seeds removed, chopped
- 1 green pepper stem and seeds removed, chopped
- 2 celery stalks chopped
- 1/2 pint mushrooms cleaned and sliced
- 14.5 oz can artichoke hearts quartered, drained and rinsed
- 1/4 cup sliced olives
- salt and pepper
- 1/2 teas oregano
- 1/4 teas basil
- 1/4 teas red pepper flakes
- 1/8 teas cardamom
- 1/4 to 1/2 cup olive oil
- 1 package Wild Garden Couscous
- 1/4 cup crumbled feta
- Few sprigs fresh parsley oregano, and thyme, minced for garnish
- Bib lettuce or Pita for serving

Instructions

1. Pat the chicken dry and place in a resealable container, coating the Wild Garden Persian Marinade. Cover and place in the fridge for up to 24 hours.
2. When ready to grill, clean the grates and allow the grill to heat.
3. Grill the chicken over indirect heat until an instant read thermometer reads 160 flipping once halfway through.
4. Wrap in foil and allow to rest, allowing the temp to rise to 165.
5. Meanwhile, slice two lemons in half and char over the flame. Remove from heat and set aside.

6. Meanwhile, toss the onion, peppers, celery, mushrooms, artichoke hearts and olives in a large bowl.
7. When the chicken has cooked, give it a rough chop and mix it in with the vegetables. Sprinkle with a bit of salt and pepper.
8. Whisk the oregano, basil, red pepper flakes, cardamom together in a small bowl. Squeeze in the juice from one lemon and add the olive oil. Stir to combine.
9. Cook the Wild Garden Couscous according to the package. And toss into the salad. Mix to combine.
10. Sprinkle with feta, and garnish with fresh minced herbs like parsley, thyme or oregano.
11. Arrange the fresh chicken salad on a platter with the charred lemon wedges. Serve with bib lettuce or pita pockets for serving as edible cups.

QUICK & EASY EGGS BENEDICT FOR TWO

Ingredients

- 3 tbs sour cream
- 2 tbs milk
- 1 teas Dijon mustard
- 2 eggs
- 1 whole grain English muffin
- few slices of ham
- 1 to mato sliced
- fresh chives snipped
- salt and pepper

Instructions

1. Whisk the sour cream, milk, and mustard in a small bowl and set aside.
2. In a small saucepan or deep skillet, heat enough water to cover eggs to a boil. Reduce the heat to a simmer. Crack the eggs, one at time in a small bowl and drop each one into the pot carefully so to not splash. Cook for 3 to 5 minutes until the whites are set and the yolks are almost set. Remove the eggs gently with a slotted spoon.
3. Meanwhile, toast the muffin. Top with the ham and tomato slices and place in the toaster oven for another minute (or under the broiler).
4. Arrange the eggs over the sliced tomato and spoon a bit of the sour cream 'hollandaise' sauce over each.
5. Get fancy and win points for presentation by garnishing with chives and seasoning with salt and pepper.

GRILLED CHICKEN QUESADILLAS

Prep Time: 5 minutes || Cook Time: 8 minutes

Course: Main Course

Calories: 324kcal

Servings: 4

You too can have flavor packed quesadillas with perfect grill marks without spending a dime at the local chain restaurants. Oh, and these taste better.

Ingredients

- 1 cup chopped cooked chicken try using leftover smoked chicken
- 8 flour tortillas
- 1 tsp Montreal Chicken Seasoning
- 1/4 red pepper diced
- 1/4 green pepper diced
- 1/4 onion diced
- 1/3 cup black beans drained and rinsed
- 3 scallions sliced
- 3/4 cup shredded cheddar cheese or pepper jack if you're feeling feisty
- Guacamole Salsa, Sour Cream for dipping

Instructions

- Preheat grill to high. Clean grate.
- Meanwhile, arrange all chicken (sprinkled with seasoning), peppers, onions, black beans, scallions and cheese evenly over 4 tortillas.
- Top with another tortilla and press to even things out and make sure the centers aren't bulging.
- Back at the grill, reduce heat to medium and carefully place quesadillas on grill.
- Press like you are making a panini. Grill 3 to 4 minutes
- Flip and continue to grill until cheese is melted and everything is heated through.
- Remove from grill, and on a cutting board, slice into even portions with a pizza cutter.
- Serve with fixins.

SMOKED CHICKEN BREAST

Prep Time: 5 Minutes || Cook Time: 1 Hour 30 Minutes

Serving Size: 1

Amazing smoked flavor on a lean and juicy cut? Chicken breast takes incredibly well to smoke flavor over fresh coals. Try this recipe & amaze your friends.

Ingredients

- 4 lbs boneless skinless chicken breast
- 1 tbsp. olive oil
- 1 tspn salt
- 1/2 tspn pepper
- 1 tbsp. sweet and spicy poultry blend of choice

Instructions

1. Pat the chicken dry and prep the grill for offset smoking aiming for a temperature of 225 to 250 by stacking the coals one side of the grill.
2. While the smoker comes to temperature, rub the chicken with the olive oil and season liberally with salt, pepper, and your favorite spicy poultry blend.
3. Once the smoker is ready, to lay wood chips over the embers and arrange the chicken on the cooler side of the grill.
4. Close the lid and allow the chicken to smoke, opening minimally to avoid letting smoke and heat out, until the chicken is cooked through, and an instant read thermometer temps at 160 at the thickest part, about 60 to 90 minutes. Flipping once if needed.
5. Add the corn the last 20 minutes or so, to allow the corn to pick up smoke flavor.
6. When the chicken is cooked, remove from heat and rest in foil.
7. While the chicken rests, finish cooking the corn, rotating, over the hot side of the grill.
8. Slice the chicken into thin strips and cut the corn in half.
9. Serve

Amount Per Serving: Calories: 566, Total Fat: 21g, Saturated Fat: 5g, Trans Fat: 0g, Unsaturated Fat: 14g, Cholesterol: 197mg, Sodium: 501mg, Carbohydrates: 20g, Fiber: 5g, Sugar: 5g, Protein: 74g

QUICK PRESSURE COOKER TURKEY BREAST RECIPE

Prep Time: 5 minutes || Cook Time: 40 minutes

Course: Main Course

Calories: 133kcal

Servings: 6

Put the pressure cooker to work for a holiday feast that comes together in under an hour. Quick Pressure Cooker Turkey Breast Recipe – 40 minutes to the table.

Ingredients

- 6 – 7 lbs bone-in turkey breast thawed
- 1 onion halved
- 3 garlic cloves smashed
- 1 carrot cut in half
- 2 celery stalks cut in half
- 4 cups chicken broth
- salt and pepper
- 1 tbsp. fresh rosemary chopped
- 1 tbsp. fresh parsley chopped
- 1 tbsp. fresh sage
- 4 tbsp. butter bonus points for herb butter
- For the Gravy
- Reserved cooking liquid from the turkey breast
- 2 tbsp. butter
- 2 tbsp. flour

Instructions

1. Place the chicken broth in the pressure cooker and add a steamer, open fully over top. Place the onion, garlic, carrot, and celery to the steamer.
2. Mix the rosemary and parsley together in a bowl.
3. Pat the turkey dry with paper towels.
4. Season well with salt and pepper (don't forget to season the cavity).
5. Carefully use your fingers to pull up the skin from the top of the turkey breast and rub with the chopped herbs.
6. Slide 4 pats of butter (about 1 tablespoon each) under the skin and a few of the sage leaves.
7. Place the turkey breast in the pressure cooker.
8. Seal the lid and set your pressure cooker to 30 minutes.
9. Allow the pressure to cook the turkey and release the steam naturally.

10. Carefully remove the turkey breast from the pressure cooker when the pressure has released.
11. Place the turkey on a baking sheet and put under the broiler for a few minutes to brown the skin.
12. Remove and wrap well to rest.
13. Remove the steamer with the cooked vegetables and discard.
14. Make the Gravy
15. Meanwhile, melt the butter in a small saucepan. Add the flour and allow to cook for one minute.
16. Ladle about a cup of the cooking liquid into the saucepan, whisking, to create a roux.
17. Add a little more liquid if needed. Once the roux has come together, set your pressure cooker to simmer and add the roux.
18. Allow to cook until thickened, 5 to 7 minutes. (If your pressure cooker does not have this option, continue to whisk the cooking liquid into the flour and butter mix and cook until thickened).
19. Serve the turkey breast sliced with the gravy on the side.

QUICK BBQ CHICKEN WITH GRILLED APPLES

Prep Time: 5 minutes || Cook Time: 25 minutes

Course: Main Course

Calories: 617kcal

Servings: 4

A weeknight quick meal that is perfect for anyone trying to eat healthy (it's Whole30 approved) and loaded with flavor!

Ingredients

For the Chicken

- 4 chicken breasts boneless and skinless
- 1/2 cup olive oil
- 2 tbsp. paprika
- 1 tsp cumin
- salt
- pepper
- For the Apples
- 2 tbsp. olive oil
- 2 Granny Smith Apples

Instructions

1. Preheat your grill for two-zone grilling.
2. Pat the chicken dry. Whisk the ½ cup olive oil, paprika, cumin, salt and pepper in a bowl. Place in a sealable bag and add the chicken. Seal bag and massage chicken to evenly coat.
3. Cook for 10 minutes or so, depending on the thickness of the chicken. Flip, cooking another 10 minutes until internal temperature reaches 165 degrees Fahrenheit. An instant read thermometer is great for checking internal temperatures.
4. Remove chicken and let rest.
5. While chicken rests, slice apples into thin wedges. Toss in 2 tablespoons of olive oil. Place apples on indirect heat of the grill. Grill apple slices, 3 to 5 minutes until just beginning to see grill marks on both sides. Remove from grill.
6. Slice chicken and arrange on a platter with the apples. Drizzle accumulated juices over the chicken and serve.

CHICKEN IN TARRAGON CREAM SAUCE WITH GREEN RICE PILAF

Ingredients

- 3 tbs unsalted butter
- A small handful of thin whole wheat spaghetti
- 1 cup rice
- 2 1/2 cups low-sodium chicken stock
- 1 cup fresh green beans trimmed
- salt and pepper
- 1 lbs boneless skinless chicken breasts sliced into thin cutlets
- 1 tbs olive oil
- 1 cup small white mushrooms sliced thin
- 1 shallot minced
- 1 tbs flour
- 1/3 – 1/2 cup sour cream or creme fraiche
- 3 tbs tarragon freshly chopped
- 1 tbs Dijon mustard

Instructions

1. In a medium saucepan with a good lid, melt 1 tablespoon of the butter over medium heat. Break the spaghetti up and add to the pan.
2. Cook, stirring a bit, until browned; 2 to 3 minutes. Add the rice and 1 3/4 cups chicken stock and bring to a boil.
3. Cover, lower the heat to a simmer, and let cook for 18 minutes or so, until most of the stock has been absorbed. Fluff the rice with a fork.
4. Meanwhile, steam the green beans and set aside. Stir the green beans into the cooked rice, leave covered and set aside.
5. While the rice is doing its thing, trim the chicken if needed and season with salt and pepper.
6. In a large skillet over medium-high heat, add the olive oil and swirl to coat pan. Add the chicken, and cook until golden, about 6 minutes per side depending on thickness. Transfer the chicken and cover while you make the sauce.
7. Melt the remaining 2 tbs butter in the now empty skillet and add the shallots and mushrooms. Cook for about 5 minutes until everything is nice and tender. Season with salt and pepper and sprinkle the flour over top. Stir and cook for 1 minute.
8. Whisk the remaining 1 cup of chicken stock (or add a splash of white wine) and deglaze the pan. Stir in the sour cream, tarragon, Dijon, and any juices the chicken may have accumulated. Whisk until smooth.

9. Serve the chicken with the rice pilaf and an allow dinner guests to spoon the sauce over top.

SMOKED ROAST BEEF

Prep Time: 15 minutes || Cook Time: 3 hours

Course: Main Course

Calories: 304kcal

Servings: 8

This smoked beef takes a classic roast to a whole new level with the sublte hint of smoke flavor and a finishing sear to lock in the juices.

EQUIPMENT

Smoker

1 10" Cast Iron pan

Ingredients

- 3 lbs round roast
- 1 tbsp. salt
- 1 tsp black pepper
- 2 tbsp. dijon mustard
- 4 cloves garlic minced
- 2 tbsp. fresh rosemary minced
- 4 tbsp. butter
- Fresh rosemary and salt for garnish

For the smoked horseradish cream sauce

- ⅓ – ½ cup heavy cream
- 1 tbsp. butter
- 1 shallot minced
- 1 tbsp. mayo
- 1 tbsp. spicy mustard
- 2 tbsp. sour cream
- 8 oz high-quality horseradish
- Black pepper and salt
- Fresh rosemary minced, for garnish

Instructions

1. Smoke the Meat, prep your smoker for indirect heat.
2. Sprinkle the beef liberally with the salt on all sides.
3. Rub the beef evenly with the mustard. Pat the minced garlic and rosemary all over the beef.
4. When the smoker is ready, add the wood chunks over the coals and place the beef over the cooler side of the grill.
5. Cover and cook the beef until it reaches an internal temp of 120 degrees.
6. Remove from heat, sear the Beef, you can add more coals to the fire and get it going for a hot fire now, or use a stovetop for the next step.
7. Place a cast-iron skillet over the medium-high heat and melt 2 tablespoons of the butter. Swirl to coat the pan.
8. Quickly sear the beef on all sides, 3 to 5 minutes per side, for a good crust over the herbs and garlic.
9. Place the beef over heavy foil. Top with the two remaining tablespoons of butter and wrap it tightly.
10. Let the beef rest for 10 minutes, to an internal temp of 135 degrees, before slicing thin to serve.
11. Garnish with fresh rosemary and serve the smoked horseradish sauce on the side.
12. Make the smoked horseradish cream sauce:
13. Place a small heatproof pan with the heavy cream in it over the grate. Allow it to sit over the heat, without simmering for about 45 minutes to an hour.
14. Stir often. Taste a bit of the cream to make sure it has thickened a bit and has a gentle smoked flavor.
15. Remove from heat. Melt butter in a cast-iron skillet over the fire.
16. Add the minced shallots and cook until crisp, 3 to 5 minutes.
17. Remove from heat, in a bowl, whisk the mayo, mustard, sour cream, shallots and horseradish together.
18. Whisk in the smoked cream a little at a time until smooth and drips form a spoon but is still thick, season with black pepper and salt.
19. Garnish with fresh rosemary minced, if desired.

NOTES

- You want to make sure the smoker is prepped and holding temp before adding your wood. Depending on the smoker, I let mine pre-heat up to an hour before actually smoking the meat.
- Between getting good embers and a stable temp, these things can take time and always depend on the weather (wind, temp, altitude, etc).
- If you don't have a chimney to light your coals, using small firestarters strategically placed in the pile of coals is a great way to light your fire. I build a pile of charcoal to one side of my smoker and nestle a firestarter or two in with a few chunks on top.

- Using a long lighter, I then light them and let the charcoal heat up and get ashen before even starting to cook.

MCCOLGAN'S SPICY KETO DRY RUB

Prep Time: 5 mins

Course: Main Course

Servings: 48 servings

Calories: 29 kcal

Looking for a delicious sugar-free, keto dry rub for your meats? This easy recipe has a delicious flavor and nothing that will wreck your keto efforts.

Ingredients

- 4 ounces smoked paprika
- 2 ounces garlic powder
- 2 ounces onion powder
- 2 ounces chili powder
- 2 ounces black pepper
- 2 ounces ground mustard
- 2 ounces celery salt
- 1.5 ounces ground red pepper

Instructions

1. Pour all of the spices into a large bowl.
2. Mix well using a whisk until spices are evenly combined.
3. Store in an airtight container.

Recipe Notes

This large batch of dry rub makes enough for about 12 racks of ribs. Unlike many dry rubs, there is no sugar added. For each rack of ribs, this recipe adds about 8 net carbs, which works out to about 2 net carbs per serving.

Calories 29 Calories from Fat 9, Fat 1g2%, Saturated Fat 0g0%, Cholesterol 0mg0%, Sodium 481mg21%, Potassium 144mg4%, Carbohydrates 5g2%, Fiber 2g8%, Sugar 0g0%, Protein 1g2%, Vitamin A 1890IU38%, Vitamin C 1.1mg1%, Calcium 25mg3%, Iron 1.1mg6%

CARNIVORE CHILI

Ready in: 2hrs 5mins

Serves: 6

Ingredients

- 1 ½ tablespoons olive oil
- 3 cups finely chopped yellow onions
- 5 garlic cloves, minced
- 2 lbs extra lean ground beef
- 2 tablespoons chili powder
- 1 tablespoon ground cumin
- 1 tablespoon dried oregano
- 2 teaspoons unsweetened cocoa
- 2 teaspoons salt
- 1 teaspoon celery seed
- 1 teaspoon ground turmeric
- 1 teaspoon ground cinnamon
- ½ teaspoon crushed red pepper flakes
- 2 cups tomato juice
- 2 cups reduced-sodium fat-free beef broth
- ¼ cup yellow cornmeal

Directions

1. In a 5-quart pan, warm olive oil over medium heat. Add onions and garlic and cook, uncovered, stirring once or twice, for 10 minutes.
2. Add ground beef and cook, stirring and breaking up lumps, until meat is evenly crumbled and no longer pink, about 8 to 10 minutes.
3. Stir in chili powder, cumin, oregano, cocoa, salt, celery seeds, turmeric, cinnamon and red pepper flakes; cook another 3 minutes, stirring often. Stir in tomato juice, beef broth and cornmeal, and bring to a boil.
4. Lower heat and simmer, uncovered, stirring occasionally, until chili is thick and reduced by one-third, about 1 1/2 hours. Taste and adjust seasonings.
5. Serve topped with shredded cheese, sour cream and chopped green onions, if desired.

CARNIVORE'S DELIGHT

Ready In: 3hrs 15mins

Serves: 35-40

Yield: 2 3/4 Gallons

Ingredients

- 1 lb. ground beef, Jim's Meat Market
- 2 lbs ground pork, Jim's Meat Market
- 2 lbs cooked italian meatballs, GFS
- 1 lb. cooked chicken
- ½ cup olive oil
- 4 white onions, chopped
- 3 green bell peppers, chopped
- 3 heads garlic
- ½ cup chili powder
- ¼ cup paprika
- ½ cup basil
- 8 cups tomato puree
- 8 cups tomatoes, diced
- 1 quart chicken stock
- 3 jalapenos, 3 (slits or side)
- ½ cup molasses
- ½ cup maple syrup
- 12 cups cooked black beans, Tenuto's

Directions

1. Cook/Brown coat meats with 2 T. of spice mix of chili powder, cayenne powder, paprika & basil (above ingredients). Set aside while preparing vegetables.
2. Saute onions in olive oil and rice vinegar until clear, add peppers and garlic and sauté till wilted. Remove from pan and add meats into remaining juices until browned.
3. Add liquid of choice, spice mix, chili base, tomato puree, diced tomatoes, and jalapenos.
4. Bring to a low boil, reduce heat to simmer, cover and occasionally stir. Simmer approximately 2 1/2 hours. Test for taste and spice "Heat". If you want less spice "Heat", remove jalapenos. If you want more "Heat", take a spoon and squeeze the juices out of the Jalapenos and leave in the Chili. Adjust to taste with chili powder and/or salt. Simmer 10 more minutes.

5. Last 15 minutes before finish, add beans, molasses, and honey. Garnish with cheese or chopped onions

CARNIVORE FRENCH BREAD PIZZA

Prep Time: 15 minutes ||Cook Time: 15 minutes

Serves: 4 People

Ingredients

- 1 loaf French or ciabatta bread, cut in half lengthwise
- 2 Tbsp olive oil
- 4 Oz H-E-B Light Sausage
- 1 cup(s) pizza sauce
- 12 Oz shredded mozzarella cheese
- 5 Oz pepperoni
- 2 1/2 Oz H-E-B 100% Bacon Pieces
- 1/4 cup(s) red onion, thinly sliced
- 8 fresh basil leaves, thinly sliced

Instructions

1. Preheat oven to 400°F. Place both half loaves on a baking sheet.
2. Place a small skillet over medium heat. Add oil and sausage. Cook sausage thoroughly.
3. Divide sauce and cheese evenly between each piece of ciabatta. Top with sausage, pepperoni, bacon and onions.
4. Bake 15 to 18 minutes or until cheese is bubbly and bread is toasty around the edges. Remove from oven and top with basil just before serving.

Chef's tip: For the same great flavors with less bread use same ingredients on top of naan bread. Cooking time will be 6 to 7 minutes

KETO STEAK NUGGETS

Servings: 4

Calories: 350kcal

Ingredients

- 1 pound venison steak or beef steak, cut into chunks.
- 1 large Egg(s)
- Lard or palm oil for frying

Keto Breading

- 1/2 cup grated parmesan cheese
- 1/2 cup pork panko
- 1/2 teaspoon Homemade Seasoned Salt

Chipotle Ranch Dip

- 1/4 cup mayonnaise
- 1/4 cup Organic Cultured Sour Cream
- 1+ teaspoon chipotle paste to taste
- 1/2 teaspoon My Ranch Dressing & Dip Mix
- 1/4 medium lime, juiced

Instructions

1. For the Chipotle Ranch Dip: Combine all ingredients, mix well. 1 teaspoon of chipotle paste yields a medium-spice version, use more or less according to your own taste preferences. I encourage you to use my homemade ranch dressing and dip mix, it's superior to any store brought version. Refrigerate at least 30 minutes before serving, will keep for up to 1 week.
2. Combine Pork Panko, parmesan cheese and seasoned salt - again use my homemade not the store bought stuff. Set aside.
3. Beat 1 egg. place beaten egg 1 bowl and breading mix in another.
4. Dip chunks of steak in egg, then breading. Place on a wax paper lined sheet pan or plate.
5. FREEZE breaded raw steak bites for 30 minutes before frying. This helps to ensure that the breading will NOT LIFT when fried.
6. Heat Lard to roughly 325 degrees F. Working in batches as necessary, fry steak nuggets (from frozen or chilled) until browned, about 2-3 minutes.
7. Transfer to a papertowel lined plate, season with a sprinkle of salt and serve with Chipotle Ranch.

Calories: 350kcal | Carbohydrates: 1g | Protein: 40g | Fat: 20g | Saturated Fat: 6g | Cholesterol: 163mg | Sodium: 335mg | Potassium: 491mg | Sugar: 1g | Vitamin A: 220IU | Calcium: 100mg | Iron: 5mg

KETO STEAK AU POIVRE

Prep Time: 5 minutes || Cook Time: 10 minutes

Yield: 1 serving

Category: Dinner

This fancy dish is an easy way to impress your family and guests.

Ingredients

- 1 filet mignon or similar steak (6 oz approx 1-inch thick)
- 1 Tablespoon (15 g) salt
- 2 Tablespoons (10 g) peppercorns
- 1 sprig of thyme
- 2 cloves of garlic, crushed
- 2 Tablespoons (30 ml) ghee, to cook with

Instructions

1. Remove steaks from the refrigerator, season with salt and let sit for 30 minutes.
2. Crush the peppercorns, using a moooo. ortar and pestle or a flat board or pan.
3. Press the crushed peppercorns onto both sides of the steak.
4. In a hot skillet, add the ghee, thyme, and garlic. When the ghee is hot, add in the steak. Cook the steak for 3-4 minutes per side. This should get it to medium rare.

Net Carbs: 2 g, Calories: 696 Sugar: 0 g Fat: 58 g Carbohydrates: 2 g Fiber: 0 g Protein: 42 g

3-INGREDIENT CRISPY KETO CHICKEN THIGHS RECIPE

Prep Time: 5 minutes ||Cook Time: 40 minutes

Yield: 4 servings

Category: Lunch, Dinner

Ingredients

- 12 chicken thighs (with the skin on)
- 4 Tablespoons of olive oil (60 ml)
- 2 Tablespoons salt (30 g)

Instructions

1. Preheat oven to 450F (230C).
2. Rub salt on each chicken thigh in the mixture and place on a greased baking tray. Make sure the thighs are not touching each other on the tray. Drizzle the olive oil over the chicken thighs.
3. Bake for 40 minutes until the skin is crispy.

Net Carbs: 0 g

Calories: 713 Sugar: 0 g Fat: 56 g Carbohydrates: 0 g Fiber: 0 g Protein: 48 g

FRENCH ROAST BEEF - COLD CUT STYLE

Prep Time: 20 Minutes || Cook Time: 40 Minutes

Marinating / Chilling Time: 2 Days

Servings: 8

Turn a simple French Roast Beef into healthy and deliciously nutritious cold cuts by simply chilling it and then slicing it super thinly.

Ingredients

- 1 French Roast (or top round or top sirloin roast), about 1.75kg | 3.85lb
- 1 tbsp. salt, I use Himalayan salt
- 1 tbsp. ground black pepper
- 1 tbsp. chopped fresh thyme
- 1 tsp chopped fresh rosemary
- 1 tsp garlic powder

Instructions

1. Mix all the spices in a small container and then rub this spice mix all over the roast.
2. Cover the roast tightly with several layers of plastic wrap and place it in the refrigerator until the next day. It would be a good idea to place your roast in a rimmed plate or baking dish to collect any eventual leakage.
3. The next day, remove your roast from the fridge and take off the plastic wrap from around it.
4. Preheat your oven to 325°F.
5. Heat a few tablespoons of healthy cooking fat or oil in a heavy skillet set over high heat. When the pan is nice and hot, sear the roast on all sides until a nice golden crust forms, about 1 minute per side. Don't forget the ends!
6. Transfer the skillet to the oven and bake the roast uncovered for about 12 minutes per pound or until a meat thermometer inserted in the thickest part of the roast reads 130°F to 160°F, depending on desired doneness - 130°F for rare, 145°F for medium-rare, 160°F for medium
7. When the roast has reached the desired temperature, take it out of the oven, return it to the rimmed plate or baking dish that you used before (make sure you clean it first) and promptly place your cooked roast in the refrigerator. After about an hour, cover your roast with plastic film and let it cool completely overnight.
8. Transfer the chilled roast to a cutting board, remove the twine, carve as thinly as you possibly can and serve as desired.

Calories: 285kcal, Carbohydrates: 1g, Protein: 51g, Fat: 7g, Saturated Fat: 3g, Cholesterol: 133mg, Sodium: 1012mg, Potassium: 831mg, Fiber: 1g, Sugar: 1g, Calcium: 51mg, Iron: 4mg

TASTY BEEF AND LIVER BURGER RECIPE

Prep Time: 10 Minutes || Cook Time: 15 Minutes

Yield: 4

Ingredients

- 1.25 lbs Ground Beef, I prefer 20% ground beef
- 1/4 lb. Chicken livers
- 1 teaspoon sea salt
- 1 teaspoon ground black pepper, you can add more if you would like
- 1 1/2 teaspoon coriander
- 1 teaspoon Poultry Seasoning
- 1/2 medium Red Onion, peeled

Instructions

1. In your food processor add your chicken liver and red onion.
2. Pulse until it's a mush.
3. Next add in the ground beef and all the spices.
4. Pulse the food processor for roughly 1 minute until the mixture is blended.
5. It will be slightly sticky so you will want to wet your hands before shaping the patties.
6. Shape the mixture into four 4" wide patties.
7. Cook/Grill patties until it reaches your desired doneness (is that a word?).
8. Enjoy on a lettuce wrap or hamburger bun.

Amount Per Serving: Calories: 396, Saturated Fat: 11g, Cholesterol: 198mg, Sodium: 696mg, Protein: 29g

CAJUN-SPICED CHICKEN LIVERS WITH BACON AND ONION

Prep time: 10 minutes || Cook time: 10 minutes

Yield: 2 - 4 servings

A simple twist on the classic liver and onions that everyone is sure to love!

Ingredients

- 1 pound chicken livers (pasture-raised or organic)
- 1 medium-sized onion, chopped
- 6-8 slices bacon
- 1/2 tsp unrefined salt
- 1/2 tsp ground black pepper
- 1/4 tsp cayenne powder
- 1/4 tsp garlic powder
- optional: 1/4 tsp paprika
- optional: 1/4 tsp dried oregano
- optional: 1/4 tsp dried thyme

Directions

1. Pan-fry your bacon in a large skillet until crispy.
2. While bacon is cooking, chop the onion and prepare the livers by patting them dry with paper towels.
3. Once bacon is crispy, remove from pan and let cool. Leave rendered fat in the pan and add onions, cooking until soft and fragrant.
4. While onions are cooking, prepare your spice mix. NOTE: the mix of salt, pepper, cayenne, and garlic mimics my all-time favorite store-bought Cajun seasoning called Slap Ya Mama. Add the optional paprika, oregano, and thyme for a blackened Cajun seasoning if you prefer.
5. Add all spices to a small bowl and mix well, then sprinkle evenly on top of all the chicken livers. Feel free to double or even triple the batch for more kick -- as written it is a mild coating. I usually double the seasoning.
6. When onions are finished cooking, remove with a slotted spoon so that you leave as much fat behind in the pan as possible. If necessary, add additional bacon fat (you've got a jar in your fridge, right?).
7. Carefully add livers to the pan in a single layer. Cook until medium rare, about 2-3 minutes per side. Then, crumble the bacon into the pan and add the onions back in and gently stir everything to combine. Cook for about 1-2 more minutes.
8. Serve and enjoy! This makes a great meal for breakfast, lunch, or supper!

PAN SEARED BEEF TONGUE

Alrighty y'all, before you gag at the sight of this beef tongue, it was AMAZING! It's got perfect ketogenic macros and is actually quite easy to prepare. Packed with micronutrients and a ton of flavor, I highly recommend giving this a try!

Ingredients for 4 Oz Serving:

- Whole Beef Tongue
- 3 cups water (if using a pressure cooker)
- 1 tbsp. olive oil (or fat source of your choice)
- Desired seasoning

Instructions:

1. Wash tongue in sink.
2. Place tongue in pressure cooker along with 3 cups of water.
3. Pressure cook on the "stew" setting for 35 minutes.
4. Allow pressure to release naturally for 30 minutes.
5. Remove from pressure cooker and skin tongue.
6. Cut tongue into medallions.
7. Season tongue with salt pepper.
8. Pan sear with olive oil for 2-3 minutes per side.
9. Eat to tongue!

Cooking Notes:

If you don't have a pressure cooker, you can accomplish this with a slow cooker or a large pot. Simply boil and then drop the heat down to a simmer. Simmer for 1 hour, per pound of tongue. For instance, a three lb. tongue would simmer for three hours (plus maybe a tad extra to be safe.

APPETIZER

CHEESY AIR FRYER MEATBALLS RECIPE - KETO & CARNIVORE

Course: Appetizer, Main Dish

Prep Time: 20 minutes || **Cook Time:** 12 minutes

Servings: 6 || 4 Meatball Servings

Calories: 461kcal

Equipment: Air Fryer

Super easy low carb recipe for Cheesy Meatballs made quick and easy in your air fryer. Great for a keto diet or a Carnivore Diet, and perfect for a Carnivore Keto Diet.

Ingredients

- 2 pounds grass-fed ground beef
- 2 large pastured eggs
- 2 ounces pork rinds
- 3 ounces shredded Italian cheese blend
- 1 tsp pink sea salt
- 1 tbsp. lard

Directions

1. Place all ingredients in a mixing bowl. With clean hands, knead the mixture until thoroughly combined.

2. Roll into balls approximately 1 ½ inches in diameter. This should make 24 meatballs.
3. Depending on the size of your air fryer, you'll cook them in batches.
4. Line your fryer basket with liners, if you use them. Otherwise, spray with cooking spray.
5. Place meatballs in the basket, making sure they do not touch each other or the sides of the basket.
6. Cook at 350 degrees for 8 minutes. Pull out the basket and turn the meatballs over. Return to fryer and cook at 350 degrees for another 4 minutes.
7. Meatballs should reach an internal temperature of 165 degrees, and then they're done!

Amount Per Serving (4 Meatballs)

Calories 461Calories from Fat 288, Fat 32g 49%, Saturated Fat 13g 65%, Cholesterol 197mg 66%, Sodium 776mg 32%, Potassium 486mg 14%, Carbohydrates 1g 0%, Fiber 1g 4%, Sugar 1g 1%, Protein 40g 80%, Vitamin A 368IU 7%, Vitamin C 1mg 1%, Calcium 144mg 14%, Iron 4mg 22%

KETO CARNIVORE MINI CORN DOG MUFFINS

These are zero carb, keto carnivore corn bread muffins with mini hot dogs (aka, corn dog muffins)! They are low carb, gluten free, and a perfect appetizer or addition to any carnivore/keto meal. There's actually no corn or corn flour in these corn bread muffins (corn free corn bread?), only healthy fats and protein.

Ingredients

- 2 oz cream cheese
- 1/4 tsp sea salt
- 1/2 tsp baking powder
- 1/2 tsp garlic powder (optional if you are sensitive, avoid)
- OOOFlavors Corn Bread drops (25-30) - optional, but provides the corn bread taste
- 2 eggs
- 10 g butter, ghee, or tallow (melted)
- 3 mini Teton Water's Ranch hot dogs
- Diced jalapeños - optional, but typically used in these muffins for a little spice

Instructions

1. Preheat oven to 350. Mix cream cheese with a little water or milk to smoothen out. Just a little - we don't want any chunks.
2. Add sea salt, baking powder, garlic powder, and oo flavoring drops. Add in eggs and stir

3. Add ghee / butter / or tallow. Chop the mini hot dogs in half
4. Spray muffin pan. Pour batter equally into 6 muffin holes. Don't put the
    hot dogs in yet
5. Bake at 350 deg for 5 min
6. Take out and place one half hot dog vertically in each. Back in oven for
    another 8-10 min - done!

MACROS per muffin (out of 6):

0 carbs | 6.6 fat | 3.4 protein

As a note, to make this recipe full carnivore, omit any seasonings that you are
sensitive to and do not add the diced jalapeños. You can also try finding a cream
cheese that is 'jalapeño' flavored, but we recommend using a raw source of cream
cheese, if possible, otherwise an Organic cream cheese.

BUTTERMILK BRINED GRILLED CHICKEN WINGS

Prep Time: 6 hours || Cook Time: 25 minutes

Course: Appetizer

Calories: 649kcal

Servings: 6

Ain't nothing like a classic wing with an amazing spice rub. And this is just that. Buttermilk brined smoked chicken wings with a spice-rubbed kick.

EQUIPMENT

- Wood Chips

Ingredients

- 3 lbs. chicken wings
- 4 tbsp. Paprika
- 1 tbsp. cumin
- 1 tbsp. Salt
- 1 tsp. Chili Powder
- ½ tsp. ground Black Pepper
- ½ tsp. Red pepper Flakes
- 4 cups Buttermilk
- 4 – 6 tbsp. Hot Sauce
- 2 tbsp. Pickle juice
- 1 tbsp. Lime juice

Instructions

1. Pat the chicken wings dry. Set aside.
2. Whisk the paprika, cumin, salt, chili powder, black pepper, and red pepper flakes together in a bowl.
3. Whisk 1/2 of the spice mix into the buttermilk.
4. Add the hot sauce, pickle juice, and lime juice.
5. Place the chicken in a large resealable container, or a large Ziplock bag and add the buttermilk mix.
6. Let the chicken sit in the buttermilk 6 to 8 hours in the fridge. If you are using a Ziplock bag, be sure to place it in another dish, no need for leaks.
7. When ready to cook, prepare your grill for smoking.
8. Remove the chicken from the buttermilk brine and allow excess liquid to drip off.

9. Sprinkle ¼ of the remaining seasoning blend over the chicken, coating evenly.
10. When the grill is hot, arrange the chicken wings in an even layer over the grate. Allow them to cook with the lid closed, 10 – 12 minutes.
11. When the chicken pulls easily from the grate, flip and rotate the wings as needed to avoid burning or flare-ups.
12. Cook until the skin is crispy, another 7 – 10 minutes, moving the wings as needed to cook evenly.
13. The wings are done when they read a temperature of 165 degrees F with an instant-read thermometer.
14. Remove the wings from the grill and place them in a big bowl. Add the remainder of the seasoning and a little hot sauce if you dare and toss the whole bowl to coat. The seasoning will stick to the hot chicken wings.
15. Serve with ranch or blue cheese on the side. And napkins.

NOTES

- It's important to temp the chicken off the heat of the grill for an accurate reading. I use an instant read thermometer, like a Thermopen to temp all of my meat for accurate reading.
- These keep for 3 days stored in an airtight container in the fridge. Eat cold, or reteah in the oven on 325 for 15-20 minutes.

BEEF TALLOW FURIKAKE FRIES

Prep Time: 10 minutes || Cook Time: 30 minutes

Course: Appetizer, Side Dish, Snack

Cuisine: American

Servings: 6

Calories: 251kcal

Every truck in Oahu has a spin on street fries. This beef tallow furikake fries recipe is my take on the best street food you can get and bring back to the Mainland.

Ingredients

- 4 russet potatoes peeled
- ½ cup beef tallow
- Coarse sea salt
- ¼ cup Furikake Seasoning
- For the Sriracha Sauce:
- ½ cup sriracha sauce
- ¼ cup mayo

Instructions

For Beef Tallow Fries:

1. Preheat the oven to 450 degrees F.
2. On two rimmed baking sheets, divide the beef tallow. Place in the oven to melt.
3. Slice the potatoes into thin shoestring fries. Arrange on to a paper toweled lined rack to dry.
4. Once the tallow has melted, carefully remove from the oven and add fries, evenly, in a single layer over each baking sheet.
5. Bake for 10 to 15 minutes.
6. Carefully remove the fries from the oven and flip on the pan using a spatula.
7. Bake for an additional 10 to 15 minutes until golden and crisp all over.
8. With a slotted spatula, remove fries and drain onto a paper towel lined platter.

For the Sriracha Sauce:

1. Whisk the sriracha and mayo in a large bowl.
2. Season with salt and pepper, as desired.

For the Assembly:

1. Scoop the fries onto serving dishes.
2. Drizzle the sriracha sauce over the fries.
3. While the fries are still moist from the tallow, sprinkle them liberally with the furikake mixture.
4. Serve piping hot.

HOMEMADE SALMON POTSTICKERS

Prep Time: 1 hour || Cook Time: 25 minutes

Course: Appetizer

Calories: 131kcal

Servings: 12

These dumplings are pan-seared and steamed for that perfect crispy bite with umami layered filling of fresh sockeye. They can be made ahead and frozen so you can grab them when the craving hits!

Ingredients

For the Dumplings

- 1 package Wonton wrappers about 50 wrappers
- 2 lbs salmon filet I used Copper River Salmon
- 4 scallions minced
- 2 garlic cloves minced
- 2 tbsp. soy sauce
- 2 tsp ginger grated
- zest of 1 lime
- 1 tsp sesame oil plus more for oiling pan
- 1/2 tsp salt
- 1/8 tsp red pepper flakes

To Garnish:

- 1 tsp Sesame seeds
- 2 Scallions

For the Dipping Sauce

- 1/4 cup Soy sauce
- 1 – 2 tbsp. Sweet Chili Sauce
- 1 tsp Lime juice
- 1 tsp Rice Wine Vinegar
- 1/2 tsp Chili Oil
- 1/4 tsp red pepper flakes if desired

Instructions

Prep the Salmon

1. Remove the skin from the salmon if needed.
2. Finely mince the salmon.

3. In a bowl, whisk the garlic and scallions with the soy sauce, ginger, lime zest, sesame oil, salt and red pepper flakes.
4. Fold in these minced salmon to combine.

Prep the Dumplings:

1. On a clean work surface, arrange wrappers.
2. Place one teaspoon of filling in the center of each wrapper.
3. Gently brush the edged of the wrapper lightly with water and fold the wrapper together, pinching to seal, making pleats if desired.
4. Repeat until all the filling has been used up.

Cook the Dumplings:

1. When ready to cook, place 1 to 2 tablespoons of sesame oil in an 8″ skillet preheated to medium.
2. Nestle about 6 dumplings in the skillet, so that they stand with the folded edges pointing up without touching one another. Crisp the bottoms, 3 to 5 minutes.
3. Carefully, because the oil will pop, pour just enough water to sit about a quarter-inch high, covering only about a quarter of the dumplings, into the skillet along the side of the pan.
4. Cover and cook another 3 to 5 minutes.
5. Remove the lid and allow the remaining water to evaporate.

Make the Dipping Sauce

1. Meanwhile, whisk the dipping sauce ingredients together in a bowl. Season with more chili sauce depending on how hot you like it.
2. Serve the potstickers with thinly sliced scallions, toasted sesame seeds and dipping sauce.

NOTES

- These dumplings can be cooked fresh or cooked directly from frozen. Add a little extra time during the steaming process, as needed, if frozen. See notes about on how to successfully freeze in batches.
- Pair these dumplings with fried rice, egg rolls or sushi.
- Finding dumpling wrappers can be tricky. I often find them in the cold cases near the tofu at local markets or in Asian markets. Make sure you grab the round wrappers, not square ones

CORNED BEEF NACHOS WITH HERBED WHISKEY FONDUE

Prep Time: 5 minutes || Cook Time: 30 minutes

Course: Appetizer

Calories: 552kcal

Servings: 4

Ingredients

For the nachos

- 1 bag frozen waffle fries
- 1/2 lbs corned beef cooked and shredded
- 1/2 cup shredded cabbage
- For the Whiskey Sauce
- 1/4 cup whiskey
- 2 tbs honey
- 1 tbs brown sugar
- 1 onion sliced

For the cheese sauce

- 3 tbs flour
- 3 tbs herb butter
- 4 oz whiskey
- 2 oz Dubliner cheese
- 2 oz Skellig cheese
- 2 oz smoked gouda cheese
- 1/3 cup milk
- 1 tbs Dijon mustard
- Additional cheese for topping
- freshly snipped parsley

Instructions

1. Prepare the waffle fries according to directions on package.
2. Meanwhile, whisk the whiskey, honey, and brown sugar in a small saucepan. Bring to a boil; reduce heat to a simmer and allow to reduce.
3. Toss in the sliced onions and allow to simmer on low until soft, 8 to 10 minutes.
4. Make the cheese sauce.

5. In a saucepan over medium heat, melt the butter and flour and cook for 3 to 4 minutes.
6. Stir in the whiskey. Add the cheese a little at a time, the milk, and the Dijon.
7. Stir until melted. Keep heated over low until ready to use.
8. Toss the corned beef with the onions in the whiskey sauce and arrange over the cooked waffle fries in layers.
9. Stir any remaining sauce into the cheese sauce.
10. Pour over the fries, being sure to give a little pool at the bottom for dipping.
11. Top with cabbage, sprinkle with remaining cheese and toast under the broiler until everything is melted.
12. Garnish with fresh parsley and serve.

KETO ROASTED BONE MARROW RECIPE

Prep Time: 5 minutes || Cook Time: 20 minutes

Yield: 2 servings

Category: Appetizer, Snack

Few things beat the flavor of roasted bone marrow.

Ingredients

- 4 bone marrow halves
- Sea salt flakes and freshly ground black pepper

Instructions

1. Preheat the oven to 350 F (175 C).
2. Place the bones marrow side-up onto a deep baking tray. Place in the oven for 20-25 minutes until golden and crispy and most of the excess fat has rendered off.
3. Season the marrow with sea salt flakes and freshly ground black pepper.
4. Serve by themselves as an appetizer or scoop out the marrow and spread on grilled steak.

Net carbs = 0 g

Calories: 440 Sugar: 0 g Fat: 48 g Carbohydrates: 0 g Fiber: 0 g Protein: 4 g

KETO NOODLES

Prep Time: 5 minutes || Cook Time: 10 minutes

Servings: 2 servings

Call them spaghetti or noodles, these are zero carbs and made with meat and are the perfect replacement.

Ingredients

- 400 grams Chicken Breast Raw chicken!!!!!
- 2 Eggs
- 1 Tbsp Psyillium Husk I use this
- 1 Tsp Old Bay Seasoning Order it here

Instructions

1. Blend all the ingredients in a food processor till you get a nice smooth chicken paste
2. Then put the chicken paste in a piping bag or even a squeezy bottle. Cut the tip of the piping bag, cut lower or higher depending on how thick you want the noodles to be.
3. Get a saucepan on the stove with salted water and bring to a gentle simmer.
4. Pipe the noodles and then allow 20-25 seconds to cook. Once the noodles cook they rise to the surface. Remove with a slotted spoon
5. Cook your favorite dishes using these noodles/spaghetti.

You can skip the psyillium husk. The noodle might be a bit denser/heavy

Calories: 301, Net Carbs: 1g, Carbs: 3g, Fat: 7g, Protein: 52g, Fiber: 2g

AIRFRYER PORK BELLY

I used pork belly from the butcher so didn't really need to be left to dry out, as opposed to packaged pieces from supermarket which may require drying out before cooking

A great tip I've read is to score the skin in the direction you plan to cut the pork belly when cooked. This allows you to cut portions with ease. Will give this a try next time.

Ingredients

- 1.5kg piece pork belly
- Table salt

Directions

1. Score pork belly and salt the skin for min half an hour or can be done the night before if kept uncovered in the fridge.
2. Wipe the salt and liquid off the skin; pat dry well with a paper towel.
3. Rub olive oil on the skin and lightly salt.
4. Cook in AirFryer at 200C for 15 minutes.
5. Cook in AirFryer at 120C for 1.5-2 hours until meat is soft and cooked.
6. Cook in AirFryer at 200C for 10-15 minutes until crackling is crispy.